D1539542

MathLand.
Journeys Through Mathematics

SKILL POWER

Essential Practice for Every Day

Homework

Arithmetic Practice

Problem Solving

Test Practice

Vocabulary

GRADE 4

Creative Publications

Writers

Julie Pier Brodie
Rhea Irvine
Andrew Kaplan
Cynthia Reak
Ann Roper
Kelly Stewart
Kathryn Walker
Meg Velez

Project Editors

Jo Dennis
Cynthia Reak
Andy Strauss
Kristin Ferraioli

Editors

Jo Dennis
Kelly Stewart

Cover Design

Joslyn Hidalgo

Production Coordinator

Ed Lazar

Editorial Development

Pubworks

Production

Morgan-Cain & Associates

Portions of this book were previously published
under the title *Daily Tune-Ups II*.

© 1998 Creative Publications
Two Prudential Plaza
Chicago, IL 60601

Printed in the United States of America
ISBN 0-7622-0452-4
        6 7 8 9 10. 03 02 01 00

Contents

Dear Student,

Skill Power is a collection of challenging arithmetic problems that may be used for class work or homework. There are some special pages that will help you practice and review mental computation ("Convince Me!"), estimation, and test-taking skills.

You'll begin each unit by learning or reviewing a few vocabulary terms and then using the words for a puzzle or an activity. During the year, you'll be solving different types of problems. After solving a problem, you are often asked to "show your thinking." That means you need to explain how you got your answer. Other questions ask how solving one problem can help you solve similar problems. Use a separate piece of paper so you have enough space to draw or write about your thinking. (Sometimes your teacher may ask you to show your thinking for just one problem.)

Even when there is only one correct answer to a problem, there may be many different ways to find that answer. Talk with your classmates about how you figured out the answers. You'll learn how to convince them your thinking is correct. Listen to their ideas. You'll probably learn other ways to solve a problem!

If you are using *Skill Power* for homework, share your thinking with your family as you solve the problems. Remember, good thinking takes time!

The Answer Is...
20
$10 + 10 = 20$ $100 \div 5 = 20$
$80 \div 4 = 20$
$4 \times 5 = 20$

True or False?
The next number in this pattern is 128.
8, 16, 32, 64, _____
16 is 2 times 8.
32 is 2 times 16.
64 is 2 times 32.
128 is 2 times 64.
True

$324 + 485 =$ _____
$300 + 400 = 700$
$20 + 80 = 100$
$4 + 5 = 9$
$700 + 100 + 9 = 809$

Dear Family,

The arithmetic problems in *Skill Power* focus on building number sense. Students are asked not only to get the correct answers, but also to explain their thinking. This emphasis on reasoning skills gives children a strong arithmetic base. These exercises also include multiple-choice and true/false problems to prepare students for the format and language they might see on tests.

To encourage good thinking, most problems ask the student to prove an answer or tell about his or her reasoning. While there is usually one correct answer to a problem, there may be many different strategies or ways to arrive at that answer. The more strategies students develop, the more efficient and confident they become as problem solvers.

You will probably find it interesting to work with your child as he or she works in *Skill Power*. Express your appreciation for the effort and thinking your child shows and for the explanations he or she writes. If your child makes an error, instead of saying "wrong" or telling the correct answer, help your child to rethink the answer.

Here is a sample of an actual response to a typical problem for the fourth grade. The emphasis is on having students find correct solution methods that make sense to them, and also to explain or show their thinking.

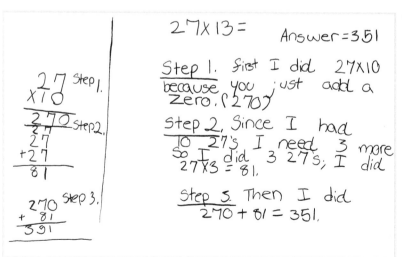

◀ This student's strategy was to break down the computation into 3 steps which she explained one by one. She showed a clear understanding of multiplication and place value as she detailed very clearly what she needed to do, and then showed her work on the side, coming up with the right answer.

Dear Student and Family,

The problems in *Skill Power* probably look like other problems you have seen before, but the way you solve the problems might be different from what you are used to doing. Below are examples of *MathLand* problems and students' thinking in solving them.

Convince Me!

You will use the "Convince Me!" method to solve many of the problems in *Skill Power*. After you calculate an answer, you explain *how* you solved the problem, convincing others that the answer is correct!
Example: The problem is 69 + 74 = _____ .

Melissa's solution:
"The answer is 143."
$$69 + 1 = 70$$
$$74 - 1 = 73$$
$$70 + 73 = 143$$

Harpreet's solution:
"The answer is 143."
$$60 + 70 = 130$$
$$9 + 4 = 13$$
$$130 + 13 = 143$$

Estimation

There are two types of estimation pages in *Skill Power* to help you build your estimation skills. Estimating before you work a problem lets you know if an answer is reasonable. What are other reasons for estimating an answer?

On "It's Between" pages, you will write two estimates, one that is less than and one that is greater than the actual answer.
Example: 65 x 8 is between <u>480</u> and <u>560</u> .
Why? 60 x 8 is 480; 70 x 8 is 560; 65 is between 60 and 70, so the answer is between 480 and 560.
On "Greater Than, Less Than" pages, you will estimate whether an answer would be greater than (>) or less than (<) a given answer.
Example: 1/3 of 19 is <u>less</u> than 7 because 1/3 of 21 is 7; 19 is less than 21, so 1/3 of 19 is less than 7.

Computation Review

These are mixed-practice pages for reviewing your computation skills. Try to solve each of the 20 problems as quickly as you can. You don't need to explain your thinking, but comparing solution methods with your classmates may give you some new strategies to use next time!

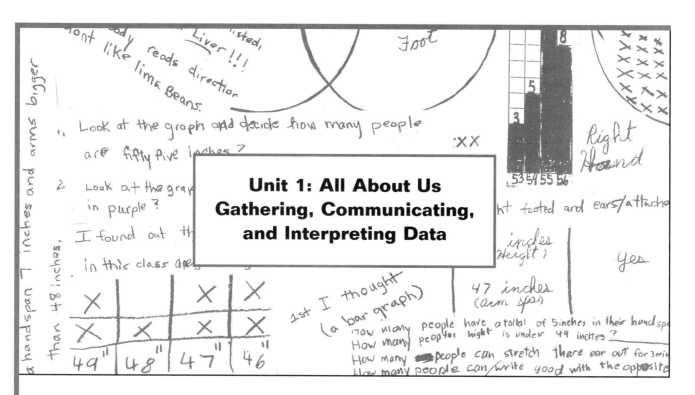

Thinking Questions

How many students in your class have the same-size hand span? Are there more left-handed or more right-handed people in your class? How do you conduct a survey? Is there more than one way to record and display information? If so, are some ways more appropriate or useful than others?

Investigations

In this MathLand unit, you will discover answers to these questions and more as your class collects data and creates graphs and diagrams to report that data. You will learn how to interpret the information on other students' displays, and you will investigate different ways to organize and report data.

Real-World Math

Watch for different ways data are used in everyday life. Some examples that you might see in the newspaper are batting averages, world temperatures, and rainfall amounts. What other ways do you find data being used?

Math Vocabulary

During this MathLand unit, you may be using some of these words as you talk and write about collecting information.

Data are facts and information.

Example: Only 3 students in my class are left-handed.

Data analysis is thinking about the data you have collected and deciding what you should do with the information.

A **graph** is a chart for showing information. Graphs have titles, numbers, and labels.

A **bar graph** compares amounts by using bars.

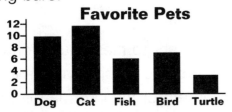

A **pictograph** uses pictures to show amounts.

May Car Sales at Best Cars

Kind	Number Sold
Luxury	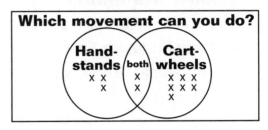
Mid-size	
Compact	

= **20 Cars**

Data on a **line graph** are represented by points that are connected by line segments.

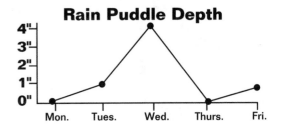

A **survey** is a way to gather data about a subject. In a survey, people answer one or more questions about a subject.

A **tally** is a notch or mark to represent a number.

Example: Carlos III
         Hyru Ⅲ I

A **Venn diagram** is a diagram of overlapping circles showing sets and the common elements between them.

Which movement can you do?

Hand-stands — x x x
both — x x
Cart-wheels — x x x / x x x / x

PARENT NOTE:
As children gain new skills and knowledge, these math terms will help them communicate what they have learned.

Digging for Data

Fill in the blanks with the correct vocabulary word.
Find each word in the block of letters. Words may go up, down, across, backwards, or diagonally.

1. Different kinds of graphs are ___*Bar*___ , _____ ,

and_____ .

2. A _____ is made up of overlapping circles.

3. _____ are facts and information.

4. A _____ can be used to gather information.

5. A _____ is a mark.

6. A chart for showing information is a _____.

7. Studying the facts you have gathered is called _____ .

```
D S H P A R G E N I L V
P A A B C D E F G A H E
R I T J K L M N O T P N
E G R A P H Q R S A T N
F U V W A X Y Z A D B D
E C D E F N G T H I J I
R B A R G R A P H S K A
E L M N O L P L Q R S G
N T U V L W X Y Y Z A R
C B C Y Y E V R U S D A
E E F G H I J K L M I M
S H P A R G O T C I P S
```

1

Solve

$$\begin{array}{r} 20 \\ +30 \\ \hline \end{array} \qquad \begin{array}{r} 2 \\ +5 \\ \hline \end{array} \qquad \begin{array}{r} 22 \\ +35 \\ \hline \end{array}$$

2

Choose the Correct Answer

$12 + 19 =$ _____

A   30

B   31

C   32

D   35

Explain how you know.

3

How Many Students?

There are 32 students in Jack's class. Of the students, 21 can roll their tongue. The rest cannot. How many students cannot roll their tongue?

Show how you know.

4

Agree or Disagree?

Maria's arm span is 37 in. She says that 37 in. is equal to 3 ft 1 in. Do you agree or disagree?

Show your thinking.

1

Find the Differences

$$
\begin{array}{r} 38 \\ -16 \\ \hline \end{array}
\qquad
\begin{array}{r} 42 \\ -20 \\ \hline \end{array}
$$

$$
\begin{array}{r} 65 \\ -27 \\ \hline \end{array}
\qquad
\begin{array}{r} 68 \\ -30 \\ \hline \end{array}
$$

How can you use the second difference in each pair to help you find the first?

Explain your thinking.

2

Choose the Correct Answer

Which 2 numbers have a difference of 10?

A   24 and 48

B   16 and 36

C   14 and 25

D   19 and 29

Explain how you know.

3

How Many Students?

There are 30 students in Helena's class. Of the students, 18 have pets. How many students in the class do not have pets?

Show your thinking.

4

The Answer Is 50

Write at least 4 different equations that have this answer.

▼ PARENT NOTE:
On these pages, students solve different types of problems, rather than focusing on one type of problem. In this way students are able to use the new strategies and mathematical thinking they learn as the year progresses.

1

Write the Answers

45 + 30 = ____

20 + 55 = ____

65 + 10 = ____

Show your thinking.

2

Choose the Answer

What is another way to write 100?

A   50 + 25

B   25 + 25 + 25

C   75 + 50

D   25 + 75

3

Who Likes Artichokes?

José surveyed his class of 30 students to find out how many students like artichokes.
One half of the students said that they like artichokes. How many students in José's class like artichokes?

Explain how you know.

4

Which Is Greater?

Write < or > in each circle to show which is greater.

130−40   ◯   135−50

170−80   ◯   180−88

220−60   ◯   230−73

Ms. Lopez's Class

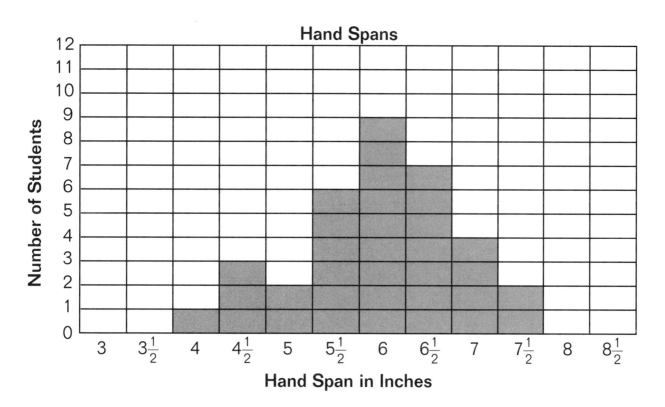

Hand Spans

1. How many students have a hand span of $5\frac{1}{2}$ in.? _____

2. What is the most common hand span in Ms. Lopez's class? _____

What is the least common hand span? _____

3. How many students have a hand span of 6 in. or more? _____
Explain your thinking.

4. How many students in Ms. Lopez's class took part in the survey? _____
Show how you know.

5. Sandra was late to class and is not shown on the graph. Her hand span is 7 in.
Add Sandra's hand span to the graph.

What's a Good Estimate?
It's Between ...

Build your estimation skills. For each problem, write two numbers, one number that is greater than and one number that is less than the exact number would be. Explain why you chose those numbers.

$$\begin{array}{r} 78 \\ -37 \\ \hline \end{array}$$

_____ and _____

Why? _____

_____

$$\begin{array}{r} 56 \\ +43 \\ \hline \end{array}$$

_____ and _____

Why? _____

_____

$$\begin{array}{r} 54 \\ -27 \\ \hline \end{array}$$

_____ and _____

Why? _____

_____

$$\begin{array}{r} 35 \\ +59 \\ \hline \end{array}$$

_____ and _____

Why? _____

_____

Maria has 49¢. She wants to buy a pen that costs 75¢. How many more cents does Maria need?

Maria needs between _____ and _____ more cents.

Why? _____

PARENT NOTE:
During the year, MathLand students will develop different types of estimation techniques. Knowing different ways to estimate allows students to choose the method that they find most effective for a particular problem.

1

Find the Sums

150	109	170
+ 49	+ 90	+ 29

Explain how you know.

2

Choose the Answers

Look at the 4 possible answers. Which 2 answers would you rule out first?

$168 - 29 =$ _____

A   99   C   149

B   139   D   161

Explain your thinking.

3

How Many Students?

Tanya and Jelani surveyed students at their school about their favorite sports. Tanya surveyed 67 students. Jelani surveyed 83 students. How many students did they survey all together? Suppose they wanted to survey the whole school of 320 students. How many more students would they need to survey?

Show how you know.

4

True or False?

$100 - 66 = 44$

Prove it.

1

Solve

199 – 70 = _____

$$\begin{array}{r} 199 \\ -70 \\ \hline 129 \end{array}$$

Explain your thinking.

I got 129 because
first I subtracted 70 from 199
to get 129. Then I just bring the
one down to get 129.

2

Choose the Answer

Choose an answer that is reasonable.

25 + 27 + 50 = _102_

A   About 75   C   Exactly 97

B   About 100   D   Exactly 112

Explain your thinking.

I added 35 to 50 also
50 + = 100 10 2 = 102

3

How Much Paper?

Mario's teacher asked him to give 2 sheets of paper to each of the 33 students in his class. How many sheets of paper will Mario need?

Show your thinking.

$$\begin{array}{r} 33 \\ \times 2 \\ \hline 66 \end{array}$$

4

The Answer Is 24

Write at least 4 different equations that have this answer.

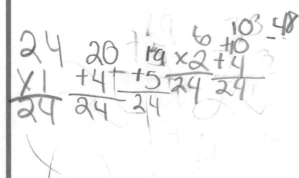

$$\begin{array}{r} 24 \\ \times 1 \\ \hline 24 \end{array} \quad \begin{array}{r} 20 \\ +4 \\ \hline 24 \end{array} \quad \begin{array}{r} 19 \\ +5 \\ \hline 34 \end{array} \quad \begin{array}{r} \times 2 \\ \hline 24 \end{array} \quad \begin{array}{r} +4 \\ \hline 24 \end{array}$$

What's an Easy Way?
Computation Review

Solve.

1. 49 + 22

2. 75 − 37

3. 33 + 51

4. 63 − 29

5. 168 + 13

6. 194 − 36

7. 4 × 21

8. 37 − 18

9. 3 × 8

Write < or > in each ◯ to show which is greater.

10. 52 + 20 ◯ 50 + 24

11. 80 − 52 ◯ 90 − 65

12. 62 + 30 ◯ 68 + 20

13. 73 − 25 ◯ 70 − 20

Circle the problems that have an answer of 55.

14. 27 + 28

15. 75 − 30

16. 83 − 28

17. 19 + 46

18. 5 × 11

19. 71 − 16

20. 18 + 38

PARENT NOTE:
As students work with computation, they will develop both paper-and-pencil and mental approaches to finding answers. As the year progresses, students continue to build their computational skills and will use those skills to solve more complex problems.

What's Your Strategy?
Convince Me!

Karen and Tyler's class solved the problem 65 + 27 = _____ . Look at their solutions. Notice that Karen and Tyler got the same, correct answer, but they used different strategies.

Karen explained her strategy.
The teacher recorded it for the class like this:

Tyler used a different strategy.
The teacher recorded his explanation like this:

$$65 + 27 = \text{\_\_\_}$$

$$60 + 20 = 80$$
$$5 + 7 = 12$$
$$80 + 12 = 92$$

$$65 + 27 = \text{\_\_\_}$$

$$\frac{-3 + 3}{62 + 30} = 92$$ Make one addend a multiple of 10.

Solve the problems below. Record your explanation on paper.

1. 77 + 19

2. 43 + 64

3. 28 + 46

4. 33 + 59

5. 16 + 35

6. 52 + 47

▼ **PARENT NOTE:**
When students are asked to explain the thinking they used to solve a problem or to find a different way to approach a problem, their problem-solving skills increase, and they become more efficient with computation.

Ted's Home Supplies

SALE!

	Regular Price	SALE PRICE!
Large Box (48 tiles)	~~$60~~	$36
Small Box (24 tiles)	~~$36~~	$18

Fill in the bubble next to the correct answer.

1. Andy buys a large box of tiles at the sale price. How much has he saved?

- ○ **A.** $96
- ○ **C.** $24
- ○ **B.** $18
- ○ **D.** $34

2. Susan buys a large box and a small box at the sale price. How much does she pay in all?

- ○ **A.** $96
- ○ **C.** $44
- ○ **B.** $54
- ○ **D.** $64

3. Juan spends $72 in the sale. What does he buy?

- ○ **A.** 2 small boxes
- ○ **B.** 2 large boxes
- ○ **C.** 3 small boxes
- ○ **D.** 3 large boxes

4. Mindy buys one large box of tiles and one small box of tiles. How many tiles does she buy?

- ○ **A.** 62 tiles
- ○ **C.** 72 tiles
- ○ **B.** 86 tiles
- ○ **D.** 96 tiles

5. Robert buys a large box of tiles at sale price. After the sale is over, he buys two more large boxes at regular price. How much has he spent altogether?

- ○ **A.** $36
- ○ **C.** $108
- ○ **B.** $90
- ○ **D.** $156

Wilson School Math Fair

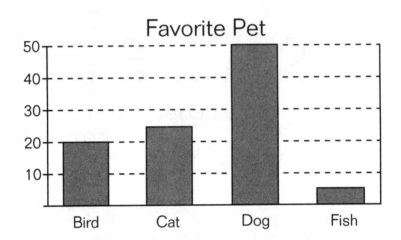

Favorite Pet

At the Wilson School Math Fair, children voted for their favorite pet. The bar graph shows the results of their survey. Use the graph to answer the questions below

1. Which pet got the greatest number of votes? Which pet got the least? What is the difference between the two numbers?

2. List the pet names in order from the pet with the least number of votes to the pet with the greatest number of votes.

3. How many children voted in all?

4. Which pet got $\frac{1}{2}$ of the total number of votes?

5. How many times more children voted for birds than fish?

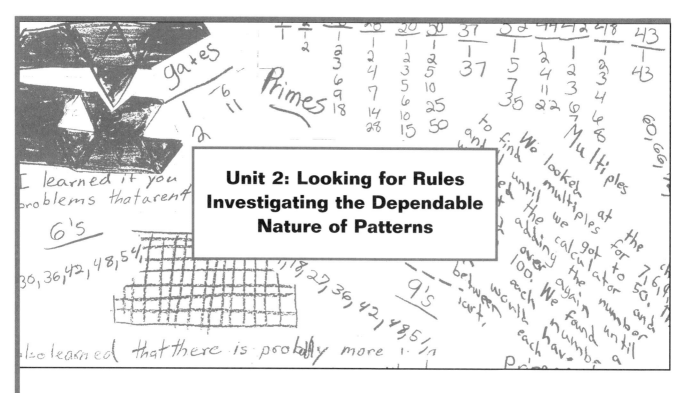

Unit 2: Looking for Rules
Investigating the Dependable Nature of Patterns

Thinking Questions

What kind of pattern can you make with Pattern Blocks? Is there a rule that your pattern follows? How can you use your rule to predict what the next block will be? Are there patterns in numbers? Can Pattern Blocks also be used to explore numerical patterns?

Investigations

This MathLand unit encourages you to find the rules that patterns follow by building and extending series of Pattern Blocks. You will also learn about factors and multiples by building rectangles that represent numbers, making a chart to organize your data, and trying to find patterns in your chart.

Real-World Math

You encounter patterns every day. Some patterns help shape your activities. Certain patterns, like bus and train schedules, help you to get from one place to another. Other patterns are useful when making predictions. Where might you find a pattern in your daily life that you use to make predictions?

Math Vocabulary

During this MathLand unit, you may be using some of these words as you talk and write about patterns.

A **pattern** is a reliable, predictable sequence or series of events. Once you figure out a pattern you can predict what will come next.

You can make a **prediction** based on what you know or observe.

Example: $\triangledown\triangle\triangledown\triangle$ is a pattern. I predict that the next shapes to follow in the pattern are $\triangledown\triangle\triangledown$.

A **polygon** is a closed figure with at least 3 sides.

A **triangle** is a polygon with 3 sides.

A **trapezoid** is a quadrilateral with exactly 1 pair of parallel lines.

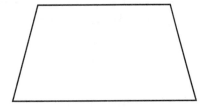

A **product** is the result of multiplying 2 or more numbers.

Factors are numbers that are multiplied together to form a product.

Example: $4 \times 5 = 20$
The factors of 20 are 4 and 5. The product is 20.

A **multiple** is the product of a given number and a whole number.

Examples: 12 is a multiple of 2, 3, 4, or 6.
Some multiples of 3 are 3, 6, 9, 12.

A **prime number** is a whole number greater than 1 whose only factors are itself and 1.

Example: 3, 5, 7, 11, and 13 are prime numbers.

Scrambled Match

Unscramble the vocabulary words.
On the line write the letter that matches the word to its example on the right side of the paper.

1. N T A E P T R

A. 1, 2, 3, 5, 7

2. A Z T R D P O I E

B. ▽○△▽○△▽○

3. D T I I C R P E O N

___ ___ ___ ◯ ___ ___ ___ ___ ___   ___ ___

C. The sun is blazing. It's going to be a hot day!

4. E I M P R   S R U B N M E

___ ___ ___ ___ △ ___ ___ ___ ___ ___ ___   ___ ___

D. 1, 2, 4, 8

5. N G T I R L E A

△ ___ ___ ___ ___ ___   ___ ___

E. 5, 10, 15, 20, 25

6. O R F A T C S   of 8

___ ___ ___ ___ ◯ ___   of 8   ___ ___

F. ⬭ (trapezoid)

7. L L U P M T E I S   of 5

___ ▯ ___ ___ ▯ ___   of 5   ___ ___

G. △ (triangle)

Arrange the letters with the shapes around them in correct order to find the answer to the riddle.

What did the factors of 8 say to the factors of 15?

"You guys  !"

1

Solve

$$
\begin{array}{r} 13 \\ \times\ 3 \\ \hline \end{array}
\qquad
\begin{array}{r} 12 \\ \times\ 4 \\ \hline \end{array}
\qquad
\begin{array}{r} 11 \\ \times\ 7 \\ \hline \end{array}
$$

Show your thinking.

2

Which Comes Next?

6, 12, 18, 24, _____

A   28

B   30

C   33

D   36

Explain how you know.

3

How Many Blocks?

Yolanda used 128 Pattern Blocks to make a fence. Half the blocks were green. How many green blocks did she use?

Explain your thinking.

4

Agree or Disagree?

Hector divided 45 Pattern Blocks into 3 equal groups. He said that there were 15 blocks in each group. Do you agree or disagree?

Show how you know.

Write the Answer

75 − 32 = _____

Explain your thinking.

Choose the Correct Answer

Which problem has the greatest sum?

A   40 + 60 = _____

B   20 + 90 = _____

C   70 + 50 = _____

D   30 + 80 = _____

Show how you know.

Agree or Disagree?

Marta's classroom has 8 tables. There is enough space for 4 students to sit at each table. Marta says that 36 students can sit at the tables. Do you agree or disagree?

Show your thinking.

The Answer Is 30

Write at least 4 different equations that have this answer.

1

Solve

$(4 + 8) \times 3 =$ _____

Show your thinking.

2

Choose the Answer

Which problem has an answer of $1?

A   25¢ + 70¢ = _____

B   85¢ + 15¢ = _____

C   50¢ + 25¢ + 35¢ = _____

D   75¢ + 35¢ = _____

Explain your thinking.

3

Which Is Greater?

Put < or > in each circle to show which is greater.

75 ÷ 3   75 ÷ 5

60 ÷ 3   66 ÷ 3

80 ÷ 4   ◯   80 ÷ 5

Tell how you know.

4

How Many More?

Ms. Chan asked each student to build a Pattern Block fence with 100 green gates. Hamid's fence has 55 green gates. Lucinda's fence has 32 green gates. How many more green gates does each student need?

Explain how you know.

Morris School Recycling Drive

Items to Recycle (full bags)	3rd Grade	4th Grade	5th Grade
Aluminum Cans	2	3	4
Glass	2	1	2
Newspapers	2	3	1
Plastic	1	2	1

Look at the chart and answer these questions.

1. Which class collected 2 bags of newspapers? _____

2. Which class collected the fewest bags of aluminum cans? _____

The most bags? _____

3. Which class collected the most bags of items to recycle? _____

The fewest bags? _____

How do you know?

4. How many bags of glass did the classes collect in all? _____

Show your thinking.

5. A bag of aluminum cans weighs about 3 lbs. About how many pounds of aluminum cans did the classes collect in all? _____

Explain your thinking.

What's a Good Estimate?
Greater Than, Less Than

Build your estimation skills. For each problem, tell if the answer will be less than (<) or greater than (>) the estimate given. Explain why you think so.

1. 4 × 12 is _____ than 40 because _____

_____

2. 60 ÷ 11 is _____ than 6 because _____

_____

3. $\frac{1}{2}$ of 9 is _____ than 5 because _____

_____

4. 16 ÷ 5 is _____ than 3 because _____

_____

5. 2 × 48 is _____ than 100 because _____

_____

Now, write a problem like one on this page.

▼ PARENT NOTE:
Developing mental computation ability not only builds real-world skills, but also lays a strong foundation for your child's future mathematics learning.

Multiply

$3 \times 24 =$ _____

Show your thinking.

Which Comes Next?

65, 50, 35, 20, _____

A   0

B   5

C   10

D   15

Explain your thinking.

Was It Correct?

Joe gave the store clerk a five-dollar bill for 2 candy bars that cost $0.75 each. Joe received $4.25 in change. Did Joe receive the correct change?

Explain how you know.

True or False?

5 ft 6 in. + 4 ft 8 in. = 10 ft 4 in.

Prove it.

PARENT NOTE:

Problems like number 4 give students an opportunity to compute in situations involving more than one unit of measure, an important skill. Showing and sharing their thinking enables students to compare techniques and learn from each other.

Name _____

Write the Answers

66 ÷ 3 = _____

88 ÷ 2 = _____

55 ÷ 5 = _____

Show your thinking.

Choose the Best Estimate

$$\begin{array}{r} 58 \\ + 21 \\ \hline \end{array}$$

A   About 70

B   About 80

C   About 85

D   About 90

Explain your thinking.

Did They Have Enough?

Mariah and Julie decided to combine their money to buy a book for a friend. Mariah had $3.50 and Julie had $2.25. The book was $5.50. Did they have enough money?

Explain how you know.

The Answer Is 10

Write at least 4 different equations that have this answer.

PARENT NOTE:
The Answer Is... problems ask students to find several ways to represent the same number. For example, the number 10 is 5 + 5, 20 ÷ 2, one less than 11, and so on.

Estimate

501
− 399

Show your thinking.

Find the Product

35
× 5

A   140

B   150

C   165

D   175

Explain how you know.

How Many Miles?

Doretta runs about 3 mi each day. How many miles does she run in a week? In a month?

Show how you know.

Does It Work?

Dom has a trick for multiplying even numbers by 5. Take $\frac{1}{2}$ of the even number. Add 0 to the end. This number is the answer.

Example: 5 × 22 = _____

$\frac{1}{2}$ of 22 = 11

Add 0 to the end of 11 to get 110.

5 × 22 = 110

Do you think Dom's trick will always work? Explain your thinking.

Equation Search

Circle 3 numbers in a row, a column, or a diagonal that form a true multiplication or division equation. There are 21 equations. Can you find them all?

12	7	27	6	81	5	28	1
5	9	4	9	36	4	54	6
3	40	9	7	7	49	62	8
7	8	80	9	8	72	3	6
21	5	8	63	42	56	8	9
3	6	10	64	4	7	24	54
48	2	9	50	36	6	6	2
5	6	30	3	32	8	4	82

What's an Easy Way?
Computation Review

Solve these problems as quickly as you can. Use the strategies that work best for you.

Write the next three numbers in the pattern.

1. 5, 10, 15, 20, _____ , _____ , _____

2. 3, 6, 9, 12, _____ , _____ , _____

3. 99, 88, 77, 66, _____ , _____ , _____

4. 56, 49, 42, 35, _____ , _____ , _____

5. 8, 16, 24, 32, _____ , _____ , _____

Solve.

6. 2×32

7. $73 - 41$

8. 3×13

9. $66 \div 3$

10. $300 - 152$

11. 9×9

12. $68 + 104$

13. 6×40

14. 48×10

15 $84 \div 4$

16. $321 + 93$

17. $763 - 96$

18. 8×11

19. $98 \div 7$

20. $407 + 264$

▼ **PARENT NOTE:**
Mental computation is a challenging activity that builds reasoning skills and number understandings. Students are challenged to solve as many problems in *Skill Power* as they can mentally.

What's Your Strategy?
Convince Me!

Robin and Mark's class solved the problem 5 × 25 = _____ . Look at their solutions. Notice that Robin and Mark got the same, correct answer, but they used different strategies.

Robin explained her strategy. The teacher recorded it for the class like this:

Mark used a different strategy. The teacher recorded his explanation like this:

$$5 \times 25 = \underline{\hspace{2cm}}$$

$$5 \times 20 = 100$$
$$5 \times 5 = 25$$
$$100 + 25 = 125$$

$$5 \times 25 = \underline{\hspace{2cm}}$$

$$4 \times 25 = 100$$
$$1 \times 25 = 25$$
$$100 + 25 = 125$$

Solve the problems below. Record your explanation on paper.

1. 8 × 22

2. 6 × 32

3. 6 × 28

4. 8 × 45

5. 7 × 40

6. 12 × 25

Ben's Building Supply

Ben's Building Supply Store puts in tile floors. This is a picture of one pattern that he puts in hallways.

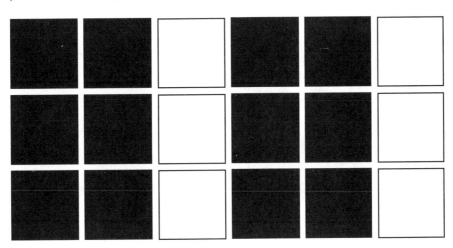

Fill in the bubble next to the correct answer.

1. Suppose Ben follows the pattern shown above. He uses 9 white tiles. How many black tiles does he use?

- ○ **A.** 9 black tiles
- ○ **B.** 27 black tiles
- ○ **C.** 18 black tiles
- ○ **D.** 36 black tiles

2. Suppose Ben uses 48 black tiles. How many white tiles does he use?

- ○ **A.** 12 white tiles
- ○ **B.** 24 white tiles
- ○ **C.** 16 white tiles
- ○ **D.** 96 white tiles

3. Ben uses 96 tiles. How many of them are black?

- ○ **A.** 16
- ○ **C.** 32
- ○ **B.** 48
- ○ **D.** 64

4. Ben charges $1.89 per tile. For the floor in the picture, which gives the closest estimate of the total cost?

- ○ **A.** 15 x $1.50
- ○ **C.** 15 x $2.00
- ○ **B.** 20 x $1.50
- ○ **D.** 20 x $2.00

5. In Ben's pattern, what fraction of the tiles are white?

- ○ **A.** $\frac{1}{4}$
- ○ **C.** $\frac{1}{3}$
- ○ **B.** $\frac{1}{2}$
- ○ **D.** $\frac{2}{3}$

The Riverside Readers

This table shows the total number of pages the members of the Riverside Book Club have read. The first day, they all read one chapter. After that, they begin to read at their own rates.

Day	1	2	3	4
Jamal	20	35	50	65
Bruce	20	32	44	56
Sarah	20	44	68	92

1. By the end of Day 4, who has read the greatest number of pages? the least?

2. By the end of Day 4, how many more pages has Jamal read than Bruce?

3. Suppose the pattern continues. By the end of Day 5, how many pages will Bruce have read? How many more pages will Sarah have read than Jamal?

4. The book is 116 pages. If the pattern continues, on what day will each reader finish?

5. Suppose another classmate also starts reading Day 1. She reads 18 pages the first day. Then she continues to read 18 pages per day. Will she finish before any of the members of the reading club? If so, who?

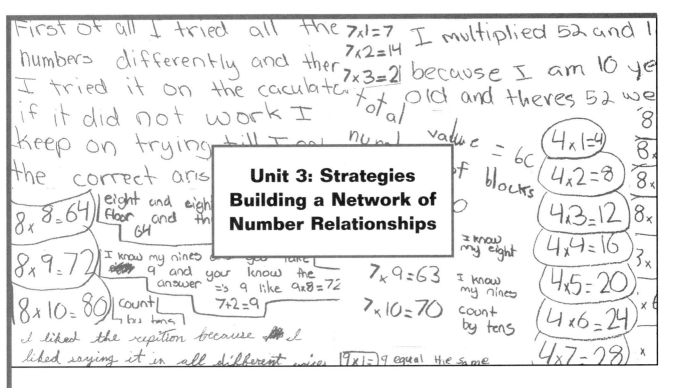

First of all I tried all the $7 \times 1 = 7$ I multiplied 52 and I
numbers differently and ther $7 \times 2 = 14$ because I am 10 ye
I tried it on the caculate $7 \times 3 = 21$ old and theres 52 we
if it did not work I total
keep on trying till I get num value = 60 of blocks $4 \times 1 = 4$
the correct ans $4 \times 2 = 8$
eight and eigh $4 \times 3 = 12$
$8 \times 8 = 64$ floor and th 64 $4 \times 4 = 16$
I know my eight
$8 \times 9 = 72$ I know my nines $4 \times 5 = 20$
9 and your know the $7 \times 9 = 63$ I know
answer =s 9 like $9 \times 8 = 72$ my nines
$8 \times 10 = 80$ count $7 + 2 = 9$ $7 \times 10 = 70$ count $4 \times 6 = 24$
by tens by tens
I liked the repition because I $4 \times 7 = 28$
liked saying it in all different ways $9 \times 1 = 9$ equal the same

Unit 3: Strategies Building a Network of Number Relationships

Thinking Questions

How much do you really know about multiplication? Are certain facts
harder to remember than others? Are there different strategies you
could use to help you remember those facts? Are there strategies to
help you solve math problems in your head? Could calculators help?

Investigations

In this MathLand unit, you will explore different strategies and problem
solving tools which will increase your mathematical power. You will
learn memorization techniques, mental math skills, and when to use a
calculator. You will gain mastery over multiplication facts, and you will
strengthen your problem-solving abilities.

Real-World Math

Having a good grasp of number relationships and mental math
strategies can be helpful in everyday life. Quick mental calculations will
come in handy whether you're at the grocery store, the movie theater,
or a baseball game. When was the last time you solved a math
problem in your head?

Math Vocabulary

During this MathLand unit, you may be using some of these words as you talk and write about solving math problems.

An **equation** is a number sentence. It includes equal values on both sides of an equal sign.

Example: $4 \times 7 = 28$

A number is **divisible** if it can be divided evenly with no remainder.

Example: 36 is divisible by 6.

A **composite number** is a number that is divisible by a whole number other than itself or 1.

4 and 12 are examples of composite numbers: 4 can be divided by 1, 4 and 2. 12 can be divided by 1, 12, 6, 2, 3, and 4.

A **digit** is any one of the ten number symbols, 0 through 9.

A **strategy** is a plan for solving a problem.

Example: Memorizing number facts is a strategy.

Double Digit Agent

Use the code to figure out the vocabulary words.
On each line write the letter that matches each word to its definition.

A	B	C	D	E	F	G	H	I	J	K	L	M	N	O	P	Q	R	S	T	U	V	W	X	Y	Z
1	2	3	4	5	6	7	8	9	10	11	12	13	14	15	16	17	18	19	20	21	22	23	24	25	26

1. 0, 1, 2, 3, 4, 5, 6, 7, 8, 9 ——

19, 20, 18, 1, 20, 5, 7, 25

A. __ __ __ __ __ __ __ __

2. a plan to solve
a problem ——

5, 17, 21, 1, 20, 9, 15, 14

B. __ __ __ __ __ __ __ __

3. can be divided evenly
with no remainder ——

3, 15, 13, 16, 15, 19, 9, 20, 5   14, 21, 13, 2, 5, 18

C. __ __ __ __ __ __ __ __ __   __ __ __ __ __ __

4. 5 x 7 = 35 ——

4, 9, 7, 9, 20, 19

D. __ __ __ __ __ __

5. a number that is divisible by
a whole number other than
itself or 1 ——

4, 9, 22, 9, 19, 9, 2, 12, 5

E. __ __ __ __ __ __ __ __ __

Use the code to solve these equations. Find the matching numbers in order to
write and solve the equation.

6. A × F = ____ × ____ = ____

7. H + P = ____ + ____ = ____

8. D × B = ____ × ____ = ____

9. Z – S = ____ – ____ = ____

10. E × C = ____ × ____ = ____

Write 4 equations using the code and give them to a classmate to solve.

1

Write the Answer

1285 + 2621 = _____

Explain your thinking.

2

Choose the Correct Answer

With which 3 numbers can you write a true multiplication equation?

A   5, 10, 60

B   16, 6, 4

C   7, 42, 8

D   7, 63, 9

Show your thinking.

3

How Many People?

A bus that seats 136 people is half full. How many people are on the bus?

Explain how you know.

4

True or False?

It takes 6 min for Toshi to jog $\frac{1}{2}$ mi. True or false? At that rate, it would take him 48 min to jog 4 mi.

Show how you know.

1

Solve

$43 \times 5 =$ _____

$46 \times 5 =$ _____

$49 \times 5 =$ _____

Explain your thinking.

2

Which Is False?

A $48 \div 8 = 6$

B $49 \div 7 = 8$

C $42 \div 6 = 7$

D $45 \div 9 = 5$

Show your thinking.

3

How Much Money?

David has 8 quarters, 70 dimes, and 20 nickels. How much money does he have?

Explain how you know.

4

The Answer Is 2

Write at least 6 different division equations that have this answer.

Find the Difference

$8.65 − $4.38 = _____

Explain your thinking.

Choose the Answer

Which problem does not have an answer of 24?

A   6 × 4 = _____

B   3 × 8 = _____

C   5 × 5 = _____

D   2 × 12 = _____

Show how you know.

How Many Legs?

Zelma lives on a farm. She has 9 dogs. How many dogs' legs are there in all?

Show your thinking.

True or False?

700 is a reasonable estimate for 287 + 316.

700 is a reasonable estimate for 432 + 266.

700 is a reasonable estimate for 392 + 375.

Explain how you know.

Crack the Code

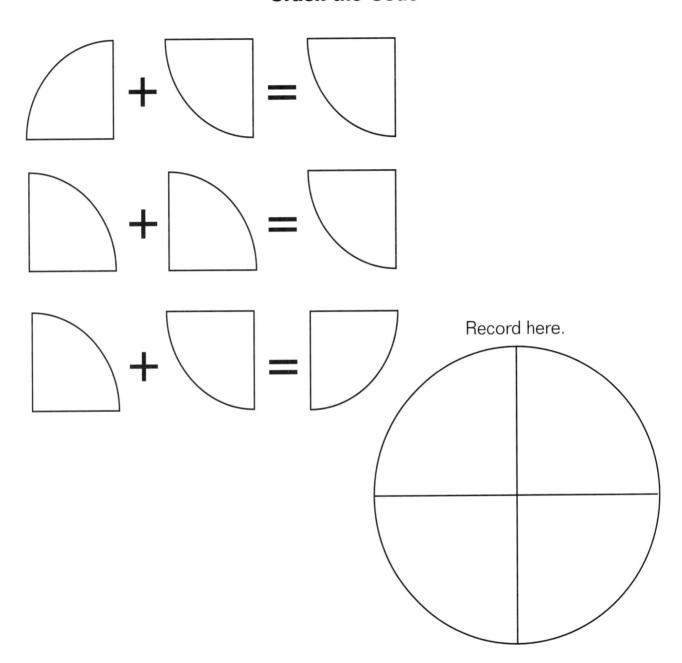

Record here.

1. In this puzzle, the symbols represent numbers. Each symbol stands for a different number: 0, 1, 2, or 3. Study the equations to decode the symbols. (Hint: Look for 0 and 1 first!)

2. Write about the strategies you used to solve this puzzle.

3. Create your own equation puzzle. Be sure to include the numbers your symbols represent. Have a friend or family member solve your puzzle.

What's a Good Estimate?
It's Between ...

Build your estimation skills. For each problem, write two numbers, one number that is greater than and one number that is less than the exact answer would be. Explain why you chose those numbers.

$$3208 \atop + 3406$$

_____ and _____

Why? _____

_____

$$63 \atop \times 8$$

_____ and _____

Why? _____

_____

9 x 36 = _____

_____ and _____

Why? _____

_____

340 ÷ 8 = _____

_____ and _____

Why? _____

_____

Thomas's class is raising money for the school. Their goal is $1000. So far, they have collected $724. How many more dollars do they need?

The class needs between _____ and _____ more dollars.

Why? _____

Multiply

```
  95
× 5
────
```

Explain your thinking.

Choose the Answer

Oak School has 200 students. Each classroom has about 25 students. How many classrooms are there at Oak School?

A 4 classrooms

B 6 classrooms

C 8 classrooms

D 10 classrooms

Explain how you know.

How Many More?

Alexis is trying to learn 100 multiplication facts. After 3 weeks of finding patterns and playing fact games, she is sure she knows 73 of the facts. How many more facts does Alexis need to learn to reach her goal?

Show your thinking.

Which Is Greater?

Put < or > in each circle to show which is greater.

$123 + 45$ ◯ $98 + 82$

$104 + 65$ ◯ $81 + 77$

$136 + 22$ ◯ $74 + 72$

Explain how you know.

1 Divide

64 ÷ 8 = _____

36 ÷ 6 = _____

49 ÷ 7 = _____

Explain your thinking.

2 Choose the Answer

Steve weighs 90 lb 12 oz. Karla weighs 5 lb 2 oz less than Steve. How much does Karla weigh?

A   95 lb 14 oz

B   95 lb 10 oz

C   85 lb 14 oz

D   85 lb 10 oz

Show your thinking.

3 True or False?

33 × 5 = 160

Prove it.

4 The Answer Is 24

Write at least 4 different multiplication equations that have this answer.

Name _____

1

Find the Product

31
× 6

Explain your thinking.

2

Choose the Answer

Rhea had $20.00. She bought a taco for $1.75 and a burrito for $3.25. How much money did Rhea have left?

A $16.00   C $15.00

B $15.25   D $5.00

Show your thinking.

3

How Many Facts?

Manuel learned 6 facts each day for 9 days. How many facts did he learn all together?

Explain how you know.

4

True or False?

$8 \times 322 = (8 \times 300) + 22$

$4 \times 116 = (4 \times 100) + (4 \times 16)$

$7 \times 463 = (7 \times 400) + (7 \times 60)$

If any statements are false, write one way to make them true.

PARENT NOTE:
One goal for students is that they learn to handle numbers in many ways. If your child is new to this approach, you can ask, "What's another way to solve this problem?"

Tricky Facts

1. What are some of the most difficult multiplication facts for you to remember? (Ones, twos, threes, fours, fives, sixes, sevens, eights, nines, or tens?) What are some of the easiest facts? Why do you think so?

2. Pick one set of multiplication facts that is difficult for you to remember. Shade every square on the chart that is a multiple of that number. For example, if you chose threes, you would shade 3, 6, 9, and so on.

3. Write about any patterns you see. Do you think any of the patterns you noticed could help you remember these facts? Explain why or why not.

Multiplication Table

×	0	1	2	3	4	5	6	7	8	9	10
0	0	0	0	0	0	0	0	0	0	0	0
1	0	1	2	3	4	5	6	7	8	9	10
2	0	2	4	6	8	10	12	14	16	18	20
3	0	3	6	9	12	15	18	21	24	27	30
4	0	4	8	12	16	20	24	28	32	36	40
5	0	5	10	15	20	25	30	35	40	45	50
6	0	6	12	18	24	30	36	42	48	54	60
7	0	7	14	21	28	35	42	49	56	63	70
8	0	8	16	24	32	40	48	56	64	72	80
9	0	9	18	27	36	45	54	63	72	81	90
10	0	10	20	30	40	50	60	70	80	90	100

What's an Easy Way?
Computation Review

Solve these problems as quickly as you can. Use the strategies that work best for you.

Solve.

1. 5×35 **2.** 4×62 **3.** 3×97

4. $56 \div 7$ **5.** $250 \div 5$ **6.** 3×141

7. 9×89 **8.** 7×48 **9.** $144 \div 6$

Write < or > in each $\bigcirc$ to show which is greater.

10. $33 \times 5 \bigcirc 35 \times 5$ **11.** $41 \times 9 \bigcirc 40 \times 10$

12. $78 \times 4 \bigcirc 78 \times 3$ **13.** $360 \div 4 \bigcirc 356 \div 4$

Circle the problems that have an answer of 96.

14. 22×3 **15.** 6×16 **16.** $104 - 8$

17. $48 \div 2$ **18.** $63 + 33$ **19.** $49 + 37$

20. $220 - 134$

▼ **PARENT NOTE:**
As the year goes on, your child will refine the strategies she or he uses to solve the problems on these pages. Students are challenged to use the most efficient method to calculate the correct answer, and to use mental computation when possible.

Solve

$9 + 9 + 9 + 9 + 9 =$ _____

Explain your thinking.

Choose the Answer

On her birthday, Marcela bought a box of 98 cookies. She wanted to share them equally among the 32 students in her class. How many cookies did each student get?

A   2 cookies   C   3 cookies

B   2 cookies,   D   3 cookies,
    4 left   2 left

Show your thinking.

How Many Desks?

There are 5 rows of 7 desks. How many desks are there?

Show how you know.

True or False?

There were 400 seagulls near the pier. Then 260 seagulls flew away. True or false? There are 240 seagulls left near the pier.

Explain how you know.

Name _____

Write the Answers

$192-88=$ _____

$194-90=$ _____

$190-86=$ _____

$189-85=$ _____

What can you say about these equations?

Write another equation that fits this set.

Choose the Answer

Which problem does not have an answer of 35?

A $5 \times 7 =$ _____

B $(2 \times 15) + 5 =$ _____

C $6 \times 6 =$ _____

D $7 + 7 + 7 + 7 + 7 =$ _____

Show your thinking.

How Much Money?

Sai had $100.00. He bought a volleyball for $22.00 and a net for $38.50. How much money did Sai have left?

Explain how you know.

The Answer Is 3

Write at least 4 different division equations that have this answer.

PARENT NOTE:
Students who learn to make sense of arithmetic start their study of mathematics on a strong footing. In *Skill Power*, your child is asked to use logical thinking and everything he or she knows about numbers to solve problems.

Find the Product

```
  80
×  3
```

Explain your thinking.

Choose the Answer

Which problem has a quotient that is less than 4?

A   35 ÷ 7 = _____

B   54 ÷ 6 = _____

C   40 ÷ 10 = _____

D   20 ÷ 6 = _____

Show how you know.

How Many Hours?

Nancy and Walter played tennis together 3 times each week for 2 h a day. How many hours did they play in 6 wk?

Explain how you know.

True or False?

Susan had 42 dimes and 16 nickels. She gave Kevin 10 dimes and 10 nickels. True or false? He has $1.50 and she has $3.50 left.

Show your thinking.

PARENT NOTE:
One of the powerful understandings students can gain is that a problem usually has one correct answer but several effective strategies for getting that answer.

Equation Puzzle

1. Use the digits 1, 2, 3, and 4 to make a true equation.

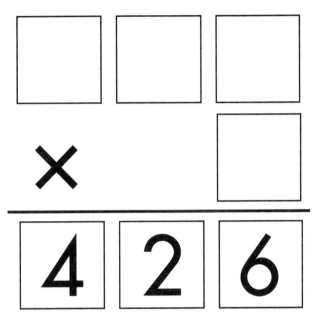

2. What strategies did you use to solve this puzzle?
Explain your thinking.

3. Write a puzzle like this for a friend or family member to solve.
Include the digits needed to complete the equation. Solve your
puzzle to make sure it works. Write the answer on the back of
your paper.

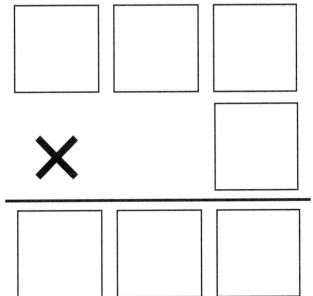

What's Your Strategy?
Convince Me!

Kerstin and Luis's class solved the problem $3 \times 118 =$ _____ . Look at their solutions. Notice that Kerstin and Luis got the same, correct answer, but they used different strategies.

Kerstin explained her strategy. The teacher recorded it for the class like this:

Luis used a different strategy. The teacher recorded his explanation like this:

$3 \times 118 =$ _____

$118 = 120 - 2$
$3 \times 118 = (3 \times 120) - (3 \times 2)$
$360 - 6 = 354$

$3 \times 118 =$ _____

$3 \times 100 = 300$
$3 \times 10 = 30$
$3 \times 8 = 24$
$300 + 30 + 24 = 354$

Solve the problems below. Record your explanation on paper.

1. 7×99

2. 6×23

3. 5×117

4. 3×247

5. 2×436

6. 4×223

▼ **PARENT NOTE:**
Students' ability to think about their own thinking, about *how they know*, is an important critical-thinking skill. Students often get clearer about their thinking as they tell about it. Take time to read or listen and respond to your child's explanations.

Solve

$235 \div 5 =$ _____

Explain your thinking.

Choose the Correct Answer

$749 + 541 =$ _____

A   1280

B   1290

C   1298

D   1300

Show your thinking.

How Many Jumping Jacks?

Roberto can do 52 jumping jacks in 1 min. At that rate, how many jumping jacks can he do in 5 min?

Explain how you know.

Which Is Greater?

Put < or > in each circle to show which is greater.

$62 - 35$ ◯ $64 - 36$

$81 - 26$ ◯ $85 - 31$

$96 - 39$ ◯ $100 - 45$

Explain how you know.

PARENT NOTE:
Fourth-graders who are new to the Convince Me! technique of problem solving might find reasoning about arithmetic a struggle at first. Over time, they develop pride in their new skills and confidence in their ability to solve problems in a variety of ways.

1

Write the Answers

$$\begin{array}{r} 89 \\ \times\ 9 \\ \hline \end{array} \qquad \begin{array}{r} 90 \\ \times\ 9 \\ \hline \end{array} \qquad \begin{array}{r} 92 \\ \times\ 9 \\ \hline \end{array}$$

Which multiplication did you complete first?
Did you use that answer to solve the other problems? If so, how?

2

Choose the Answer

Which problem has a difference of 15?

A   80 − 60 = _____

B   85 − 65 = _____

C   80 − 55 = _____

D   80 − 65 = _____

Explain how you know.

3

True or False?

44 ÷ 11 has a greater quotient than 54 ÷ 9.

Show your thinking.

4

The Answer Is 60

Write at least 6 different equations that have this answer.

1 Which Sum Is Greater?

84 + 26 = _____

98 + 16 = _____

Explain your thinking.

2 Choose the Correct Answer

Which problem has a product greater than 100?

A   5 × 15 = _____

B   5 × 20 = _____

C   7 × 16 = _____

D   3 × 30 = _____

Explain how you know.

3 How Much Money?

Yang paid $72 for 8 T-shirts. Each shirt was the same price. How much money did each shirt cost?

Show your thinking.

4 True or False?

10 × 30 = 300

20 × 30 = 600

30 × 30 = 9000

If any statements are false, change them to true statements.

Agree or Disagree?

This is how Nakesh solved the problem:

Tyler has 8 quarters, 20 dimes, and 15 nickels. True or false? Tyler has $4.50. Explain your thinking.

Do you agree or disagree with his answer?

FALSE

It cannot be $4.50 becase
if there is an even number
of quarters and dimes + 75¢ (an odd number)
it can't be $450 because it is even!

Name _____

What's a Good Estimate?
Greater Than, Less Than

Build your estimation skills. For each problem, tell if the answer will be less than (<)
or greater than (>) the estimate given. Explain why you think so.

1. 246 ÷ 6 is _____ than 40 because _____

_____

2. 5 × 18 is _____ than 100 because _____

_____

3. 3 × 48 is _____ than 150 because _____

_____

4. 108 ÷ 2 is _____ than 50 because _____

_____

5. 8 × 42 is _____ than 330 because _____

Now, write a problem like one on this page.

1

Find the Difference

279 − 80 = _____

Explain your thinking.

2

Choose the Answer

How many wheels are there all together on 4 cars and 3 bicycles?

A   7 wheels

B   14 wheels

C   22 wheels

D   25 wheels

Show your thinking.

3

How Many Feet?

Dae-Ho's playhouse is 108 in. long and 60 in. wide. How many feet long and how many feet wide is Dae-Ho's playhouse?

Explain how you know.

4

True or False?

Antonia writes to her friend about 8 times each year. True or false? Antonia has written about 24 letters to her friend over the last 4 years.

Show how you know.

Find the Products

$50 \times 50 =$ _____

$20 \times 20 =$ _____

$80 \times 80 =$ _____

Explain your thinking.

Choose the Correct Answer

$6 \overline{)420}$

A   7

B   70

C   72

D   700

Show your thinking.

Do They Have Enough?

Naoya has $32.08 and Heather has $4.79. Do they have enough money in all to buy a computer game for $36.80?

Explain how you know.

The Answer Is 4

Write at least 4 different division equations that have this answer.

Name _____

1

Find the Quotient

$810 \div 9 =$ _____

Explain your thinking.

2

Choose the Answer

Which problem has an answer of 100?

A $5 \times 22 =$ _____

B $5 \times 25 =$ _____

C $1,000 \div 10 =$ _____

D $10,000 \div 10 =$ _____

Show your thinking.

3

What Comes Next?

Write the next 3 numbers in this pattern.

425, 350, 275, _____ , _____ ,

_____

Explain how you know.

4

True or False?

These equations have the same answer.

$(9 \times 7) \times 2 =$ _____

$9 \times (7 \times 2) =$ _____

What can you say about multiplying a series of numbers?

Name _____

Dot-to-Dot Division

Solve each problem. Then write the letter of the problem on the line above its answer. Connect the dots in the same order as the letters appear.

A. $10 \div 5 =$ _____   **B.** $80 \div 8 =$ _____   **C.** $30 \div 2 =$ _____

D. $3 \div 1 =$ _____   **E.** $63 \div 9 =$ _____   **F.** $28 \div 2 =$ _____

G. $20 \div 4 =$ _____   **H.** $9 \div 9 =$ _____   **I.** $11 \div 1 =$ _____

J. $72 \div 9 =$ _____   **K.** $24 \div 2 =$ _____   **L.** $40 \div 10 =$ _____

M. $26 \div 2 =$ _____   **N.** $72 \div 8 =$ _____   **O.** $60 \div 10 =$ _____

__ __ __ __ __ __ __ __ __ __ __ __ __ __ __
1　2　3　4　5　6　7　8　9　10　11　12　13　14　15

What's an Easy Way?
Computation Review

Solve these problems as quickly as you can. Use the strategies that work best for you.

Solve.

1. 480 ÷ 6   **2.** 36 ÷ 3   **3.** 84 ÷ 2

4. 6 × 65   **5.** 63 ÷ 9   **6.** 420 ÷ 7

7. 40 × 3   **8.** 3 × 26   **9.** 360 ÷ 6

Write the next three numbers in the pattern.

10. 450, 405, 360, _____ , _____ , _____

11. 330, 360, 390, _____ , _____ , _____

12. 112, 224, 336, _____ , _____ , _____

13. 608, 532, 456, _____ , _____ , _____

14. 90, 180, 270, _____ , _____ , _____

Match each problem with the problem in the box that has the same answer.

15. 480 ÷ 6   **16.** 780 ÷ 10   **17.** 52 ÷ 2

18. 630 ÷ 3   **19.** 88 ÷ 4   **20.** 330 ÷ 11

78 − 52	66 − 44	42 + 36
42 × 5	8 × 10	96 − 66

Paul's Puppets

Paul makes puppets. He travels from town to town giving puppet shows. The map shows some towns that he visits.

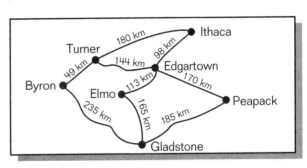

Fill in the bubble next to the correct answer.

1. Paul travels from Peapack to Gladstone. He then travels to Byron. How many kilometers is that?

- ○ **A.** 310
- ○ **C.** 320
- ○ **B.** 410
- ○ **D.** 420

2. Suppose Paul takes the shortest route from Edgartown to Gladstone. He travels 4 hours. Which gives the closest estimate of the number of kilometers he traveled per hour?

- ○ **A.** 70
- ○ **C.** 80
- ○ **B.** 85
- ○ **D.** 90

3. Paul spends a total of 7 hours driving from Peapack to Gladstone to Byron. About how many kilometers does he travel per hour?

- ○ **A.** 60 kilometers
- ○ **B.** 70 kilometers
- ○ **C.** 65 kilometers
- ○ **D.** 75 kilometers

4. Paul starts at Byron. He travels to Turner. Then he travels to Edgartown and Ithaca. Which gives the closest estimate of the total number of kilometers he travels?

- ○ **A.** 40 + 140 + 90
- ○ **B.** 50 + 140 + 100
- ○ **C.** 40 + 140 + 100
- ○ **D.** 50 + 150 + 100

5. About how many kilometers is the shortest route from Edgartown to Gladstone? Round to the nearest ten.

- ○ **A.** 270 kilometers
- ○ **B.** 350 kilometers
- ○ **C.** 280 kilometers
- ○ **D.** 360 kilometers

PARENT NOTE:
Becoming successful in a test-taking situation often involves learning how to interpret what a question is asking. This type of page gives your child that kind of practice.

Sale Days

This sign shows prices at Awesome Al's Audio and Video.

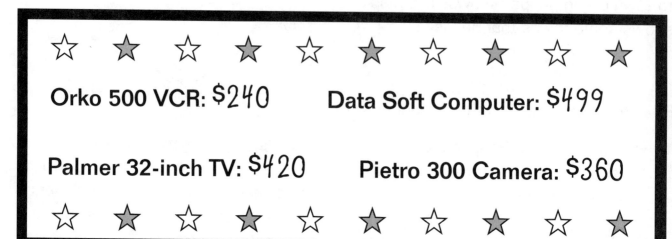

Orko 500 VCR: $240   Data Soft Computer: $499

Palmer 32-inch TV: $420   Pietro 300 Camera: $360

1. Muriel and her 2 brothers buy a VCR. They split the cost evenly. How much do they each pay?

2. Kazuo is saving money for a camera. He thinks he can save the whole cost in 6 weeks. He plans to save the same amount each week. How much money does he plan to save per week?

3. Kate has $900. Does she have enough money to buy any two items listed in the sign? Explain.

4. Good-Deal Dan's sells many of the same items that are at Awesome Al's. Dan usually sells the Palmer 32-inch TV for $480. Today he is having a sale where he takes $\frac{1}{10}$ of the price off. Which store has the better deal? What is the difference in price?

5. On Monday, 6 people buy VCRs, 10 buy cameras, 2 buy computers, and 6 buy televisions. What fraction of the people buy computers? What fraction of the people buy VCRs?

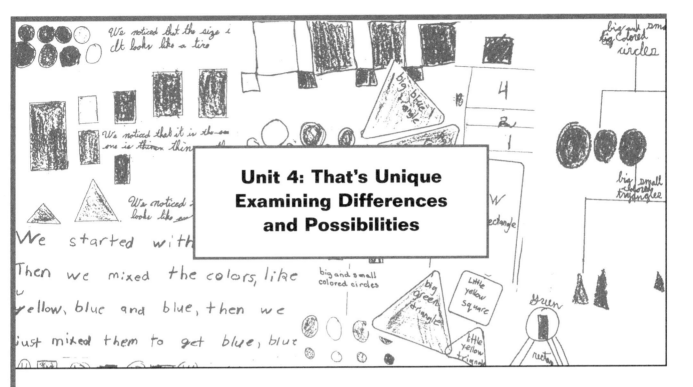

Thinking Questions

How are a large red square and a large red triangle the same? How are they different? What about a large red square and a small blue square? How many ways can two objects differ? Is there a limit to the possibilities?

Investigations

In this MathLand unit, you will learn about differences as you use color, shape, and size to analyze and compare attribute pieces. You will also get practice in thinking logically by using Rainbow Cubes to explore the limits of the solutions to combination problems.

Real-World Math

Look for the many ways that finding differences and logical thinking are used in everyday life. You might find them in the computer programs that you use or in the games that you play. Where else might you use logical thinking?

Math Vocabulary

During this MathLand unit, you may be using some of these words as you talk and write about logical thinking.

An **attribute** is a characteristic of a person or thing. An **attribute set** shows all the different combinations you can make with a certain set of characteristics, such as size, shape, or color.

Example: At the party store, you see red, yellow, and blue balloons. Some of the balloons filled with air are large and round and some are long and narrow. What is the attribute set of all the different balloons you can buy today?

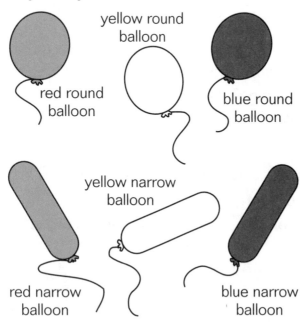

red round balloon

yellow round balloon

blue round balloon

yellow narrow balloon

red narrow balloon

blue narrow balloon

Unique means the only one of its kind.

Example: Each person is unique. No two people are exactly alike, even identical twins.

When some characteristic of an object is unlike another object in size, shape, amount, or quality, they have **differences** and are different from each other.

When two objects share one or more characteristics, such as size, shape, or amount, they share **similarities**.

Logic is a way to think about and draw conclusions from facts you know are true. In this unit, you use logic as you identify unique qualities and look for differences among members of a set.

Similarities and Differences

Read the description of each set and write down the similarity they share.

1. beach ball, balloon, an orange: _____

_____

2. rose, daisy, tulip: _____

_____

3. American flag, stop sign, candy cane: _____

_____

4. drinking glass, vase, bathtub: _____

_____

Read the description of each set and circle the item that does not belong.

5. 25, 15, 50, 51

6. seashell, nest, cave, cloud

7. jam, butter, toast, peanut butter

8. 12 − 5, 6 + 1, 3 × 4, 21 ÷ 3

9. Write out 4 sets, each with similarities or differences, and ask a classmate to solve them.

Add

$1.73
+ 0.46

Explain your thinking.

Choose the Answer

Which problem has a product of 200?

A $3 \times 100 =$ _____

B $8 \times 25 =$ _____

C $20 \times 20 =$ _____

D $6 \times 30 =$ _____

Explain how you know.

How Many Rides?

Each person needs 4 tickets to ride the Super Time Traveler. You have 48 tickets. How many times can you ride the Super Time Traveler?

Show your thinking.

Agree or Disagree?

Drew says that $\frac{1}{4}$ is greater than $\frac{1}{2}$ because 4 is greater than 2. Do you agree or disagree?

Show how you know.

Name _____

Find the Quotients

$$3\overline{)396} \qquad 2\overline{)224} \qquad 5\overline{)505}$$

Show your thinking.

Choose the Answers

Look at the 4 possible answers. Which 2 answers would you rule out first?

169 + 81 = _____

A   190   C   250

B   240   D   295

Explain your thinking.

Does He Have Enough?

Sing needs 18 eggs to make 6 cakes for the fourth-grade bake sale. He has 2 dozen eggs. Does he have enough eggs?

Explain how you know.

The Quotient Is 5

Write at least 4 different equations that have this quotient.

1

Write the Answer

640
×   4

Explain your thinking.

2

Which Comes Next?

16, 24, 32, _____

A   36

B   38

C   40

D   48

Explain how you know.

3

How Many Points?

A touchdown in football is worth 6 points. Jon scored 18 touchdowns this season. How many points did Jon score?

Show your thinking.

4

True or False?

5 × 48 > 150

4 × 49 > 150

3 × 50 > 150

What do you notice about these statements?

The Sardini Brothers

These are the Sardini brothers—Sal, Sid, Sy, Scott, and Joe.
Read the clues. Write the name of each brother on the correct line.

_____   _____   _____   _____   _____

Scott is between two brothers who have curly hair.

Joe loves his neck scarf.

Sy likes to wear stripes.

Sid is not next to Sal, who is not wearing a tie.

Name _____

What's a Good Estimate?
It's Between ...

Build your estimation skills. For each problem, write two numbers, one number that is greater than and one number that is less than the exact answer would be. Explain why you chose those numbers.

$3.25
+ 4.19
_____

_____ and _____

Why? _____

_____

635
× 9
_____

_____ and _____

Why? _____

_____

$6.25 − $3.64 = _____

_____ and _____

Why? _____

_____

144 ÷ 6 = _____

_____ and _____

Why? _____

_____

There are 195 students. They each need a red pencil. Red pencils come in packs of 6. How many packs does the school need?

The school needs between _____ and _____ packs.

Why? _____

▼ PARENT NOTE:
When students write about their strategies, they have opportunities to clarify their thinking and practice communicating their ideas to others.

Subtract

80 − 40 = _____

79 − 39 = _____

78 − 38 = _____

Explain your thinking.

Choose the Answer

Mr. Contreras bought 5 gal of apple cider. How many quarts of cider did he buy?
Hint: 4 quarts = 1 gallon

A   15 qt

B   20 qt

C   24 qt

D   25 qt

Show your thinking.

What Is the Diameter?

The Earth's diameter is 7926 mi. The diameter of Venus is about 400 mi less than the Earth's diameter. What is the approximate diameter of Venus?

Explain how you know.

True or False?

Abraham Lincoln lived from 1809 until 1865. True or false? Lincoln lived for about 56 years.

Show how you know.

1

Find the Product

$1.50
×   6

Explain your thinking.

2

Choose the Best Estimate

142 + 151 = _____

A   More than 250

B   Between 250 and 275

C   Between 275 and 300

D   More than 300

Show your thinking.

3

True or False?

121 ÷ 11 = 11

Prove it.

4

The Answer Is 40

Write at least 6 different
equations that have this answer.

Solve

Write the answer.

7 qt = _____ c

Show your thinking.

Choose the Answer

Which has the greatest quotient?

A   56 ÷ 8 = _____

B   81 ÷ 9 = _____

C   49 ÷ 7 = _____

D   44 ÷ 4 = _____

Explain your thinking.

How Many Years?

Melina is 108 mo old. How many years old is Melina?

Explain your thinking.

True or False?

72 mo = 6 yr

36 mo = 3 yr

360 mo = 10 yr

If any statements are false, change them to true statements.

Show your thinking.

PARENT NOTE:
Throughout *Skill Power*, problems such as number 4 are presented to develop students' understanding of patterns and relationships, and their ability to use patterns to check computation.

Name _____

Toby's Toy Town

Toby owns Toby's Toy Town. He uses a balance scale to figure the cost of each toy. Toby does not use the scale to weigh the toys. Instead he uses the scale in his own special way to help him figure the price of each toy. Can you figure out how Toby's balance system works? One example is done for you.

Example:

    1 bunny + 1 glove = 5 soccer balls

    1 bunny = 2 soccer balls

    1 glove = 3 soccer balls

1. 1 Ferris wheel + 1 car = 8 pinwheels

    3 cars = 9 pinwheels

    1 Ferris wheel = _____ pinwheels

2. 1 tennis racquet + 1 helicopter = 3 bunnies

    2 tennis racquets = 2 bunnies

    1 helicopter = _____ bunnies

3. 2 kites + 4 soccer balls = 6 baseball bats

    2 soccer balls = 1 baseball bat

    1 kite = _____ baseball bats

4. Challenge yourself to create your own puzzle! Show the solution.

What's an Easy Way?
Computation Review

Solve these problems as quickly as you can. Use the strategies that work best for you.

Solve.

1. 8×20

2. $448 \div 4$

3. 4×530

4. $9 \times \$1.20$

5. $275 \div 11$

6. $7 \times \$2.30$

7. $168 \div 14$

8. $\$1.35 + \$3.75$

9. 5×630

Write < or > in each $\bigcirc$ to show which is greater.

10. $140 \div 10$ $\bigcirc$ $150 \div 10$

11. 8×32 $\bigcirc$ 7×33

12. $520 \div 5$ $\bigcirc$ $500 \div 4$

13. 96×4 $\bigcirc$ 97×3

Circle the problems that have an answer of 66.

14. $606 \div 10$

15. 3×22

16. $45 + 31$

17. $330 \div 5$

18. $132 - 66$

19. $726 \div 12$

20. 6×12

▼ **PARENT NOTE:**
Learning to communicate one's thinking and to consider other students' strategies are skills that students will develop throughout the year as they write about and discuss their ways of solving computation problems.

What's Your Strategy?
Convince Me!

Roy and Yolanda's class solved the problem 128 − 85 = _____ . Look at their solutions. Notice that Roy and Yolanda got the same, correct answer, but they used different strategies.

Roy explained his strategy.
The teacher recorded it for the class like this:

Yolanda used a different strategy.
The teacher recorded her explanation like this:

128 − 85 = _____

85 + 15 = 100
28 more makes 128.
28 + 15 = 43
So 128 − 85 = 43

128 − 85 = _____

Count back by tens from 128:
118, 108, 98, 88. That's 40.
Counting back 3 more
to get 85.
So, 128 − 85 = 43

Solve the problems below. Record your explanation on paper.

1. 156 − 92

2. 133 − 79

3. 115 − 47

4. 141 − 55

5. 121 − 73

6. 175 − 96

What's the Combination?

BONITA'S BORDER • THE SNACK SHACK

FOOD		DRINKS		
			Small	Large
TURKEY BURGER	$4.95	JUICE	$1.89	$2.79
OTHER SANDWICHES	$3.79	SODA	$1.29	$1.69
SUPER SALAD	$3.19			
TERRIFIC TACO	$1.49			

Use the menu to answer the following questions. Fill in the bubble next to the correct answer.

1. Kathy has $6.50. Which combination can she *not* buy?

○   **A.**   1 turkey burger, 1 small soda

○   **B.**   1 Terrific Taco, 1 Super Salad, 1 large soda

○   **C.**   2 Terrific Tacos, 1 large juice

○   **D.**   1 sandwich, 1 Terrific Taco, and 1 small soda

2. Nora buys a turkey burger, a Super Salad, and a small juice. Which gives the closest estimate of the total cost?

○   **A.** $4.00 + $3.00 + $1.00

○   **B.** $5.00 + $4.00 + $2.00

○   **C.** $5.00 + $3.00 + $2.00

○   **D.** $5.00 + $4.00 + $3.00

3. About how much do 2 sandwiches and 2 small sodas cost? Round to the nearest dollar.

○   **A.** $10.00   ○   **C.** $11.00

○   **B.** $12.00   ○   **D.** $14.00

4. Suppose you order one food item and one drink. How many different combinations can you make?

○   **A.**   12   ○   **C.**   16

○   **B.**   24   ○   **D.**   32

5. Suppose Bonita added one more food item to the menu. If you ordered one food item and one drink, how many different combinations could you make?

○   **A.**   12   ○   **C.**   16

○   **B.**   20   ○   **D.**   32

What's the Combination?

The Animal Park uses tokens instead of money.

1 lion = 2 tigers

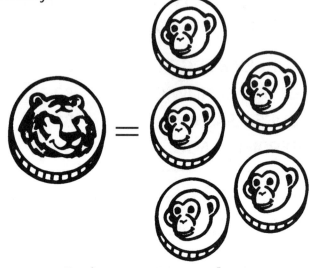

1 tiger = 5 monkeys

1. How many monkey tokens is 1 lion token worth?

2. The jungle ride costs 12 monkey tokens. What are three other combinations of tokens you could use to pay for the ride?

3. Suppose you buy a dolphin keychain. You pay with 6 tiger tokens. You get 2 monkey tokens in change. How many monkey tokens did the keychain cost?

4. The Animal Park has another token, the toucan.

How many monkey tokens is one toucan token worth?

5. A Lion Book costs 81 monkey tokens. You pay only with lion tokens. What are two combinations of change that you could get?

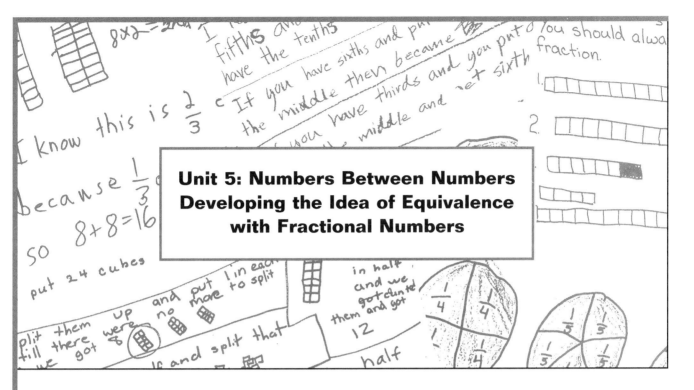

Thinking Questions

Which is more food, $\frac{1}{2}$ of a blueberry pie or $\frac{1}{4}$ of a large pizza? Would your answer change if you used a small pizza instead of a large one? What does $\frac{1}{8}$ of a circle look like? How about $\frac{1}{10}$? Can you make $\frac{1}{10}$ out of eighths? How would you add $\frac{1}{6}$ and $\frac{1}{2}$?

Investigations

By answering these questions and others, you will explore the world of fractions. Throughout this MathLand unit, you will have the chance to model fractional parts, using both Fraction Circles and everyday objects like cars and crackers. Modeling fractions will help you to learn how fractions are related to each other, the equivalence of fractions, and fraction addition and subtraction.

Real-World Math

Fractions are an important part of your daily activities. The supermarket is full of fractions: $\frac{1}{2}$ gallon, $\frac{1}{4}$ pound, $1\frac{1}{2}$ dozen. Whenever you buy or sell something, you may work with fractions, such as a dollar and a half. In what other activities might you find fractions being used?

Math Vocabulary

During this MathLand unit, you may be using some of these words as you talk and write about fractions.

A **fraction** is a number. It tells how many equal parts of a whole you are naming.

Examples: Three fourths (or three of the four parts) of the pizza is left. Fractions are written like this: $\frac{1}{4}$, $\frac{2}{3}$, $\frac{4}{6}$.

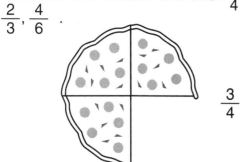

$\frac{3}{4}$

The **numerator** is the top number of a fraction. It means the number of equal parts you have.

The **denominator** is the bottom number of a fraction. It means the number of equal parts something is divided into.

$\frac{1}{3}$ numerator
denominator

Whole numbers are the same as the numbers you use for counting, starting with zero. 0, 1, 2, 3, 4, 5, 6 ... and so on.

Equivalent fractions are fractions that are equal or have the same value.

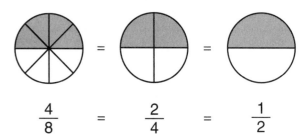

$\frac{4}{8}$ = $\frac{2}{4}$ = $\frac{1}{2}$

An **improper fraction** is a fraction in which the numerator is larger than the denominator.

Examples: $\frac{12}{6}$, $\frac{5}{4}$, $\frac{9}{5}$

A **mixed number** is a whole number and a fraction.

Examples: $3\frac{1}{2}$, $1\frac{1}{3}$, $12\frac{3}{5}$

▼ **PARENT NOTE:**
As the students learn new ideas and strategies in math, the vocabulary words give them new ways to express those ideas and strategies.

Fraction Action

Use the clues and the words in the word bank to solve the word puzzle.

Word Bank

- challenge
- denominator
- equivalent
- fourth
- fraction
- half
- improper fraction
- mixed number
- nine
- numerator
- third
- whole number

Across

2. $1\frac{1}{3}$ is called a ___.

3. the top number of a fraction

4. ⊕ = one/___.

6. 2 is an example of a ___.

8. not a whole number

9. adding fractions can be a ___.

10. fractions that have the same value

11. the bottom number of a fraction

Down

1. fractions where the numerator is greater than the denominator

3. $\frac{7}{7}$ = ___/9.

5. ◐ = one/___.

7. ◑ = one/___.

Write the Answer

$\frac{1}{2}$ of 32 = _____

Show your thinking.

Choose the Answer

15 ÷ 2 = _____

A   6 R3

B   7 R1

C   7 R2

D   8 R1

Explain your thinking.

Bus Passengers

There are 20 people on a bus. At the next stop, 7 people get on and 9 people get off. At the next stop, 4 people get on and 6 people get off. How many people are left on the bus?

Explain how you know.

True or False?

3 t = 4000 lb
Hint: 1 ton = 2000 pounds

Show how you know.

Name _____

Find the Product

$$359$$
$$\times \quad 7$$

Show your thinking.

Choose the Correct Answer

What fraction of 28 is 7?

A $\frac{1}{6}$

B $\frac{1}{4}$

C $\frac{1}{3}$

D $\frac{1}{2}$

Explain how you know.

How Much Change?

Sandy bought a candy bar for $0.65 and a magazine for $2.95. He paid with a ten-dollar bill. How much change did Sandy receive?

Explain your thinking.

4

The Answer Is 45

Write at least 6 different equations that have this answer.

PARENT NOTE:
Throughout *Skill Power*, problems such as number 3 are presented so that students can practice using arithmetic in real-life types of situations.

1

Write the Answer

$\frac{1}{3}$ of 18 = _____

Explain your thinking.

2

Which Is False?

A   70 ÷ 7 = 10

B   77 ÷ 7 = 11

C   49 ÷ 7 = 7

D   63 ÷ 7 = 8

Show your thinking.

3

How Old Is She?

Ms. Char was born in 1949. How old is she now?

Explain how you know.

4

True or False?

$\frac{2}{5} > \frac{2}{3}$

$\frac{3}{5} > \frac{3}{4}$

$\frac{5}{7} > \frac{5}{8}$

If any of the statements are false, change them to true statements.

Explain how you know.

Name That Fraction

Write the fraction of each shape that is shaded.
Can you write more than one name for each fraction?

1.

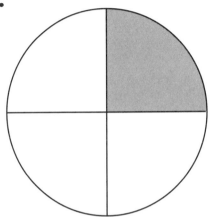

_____

2.

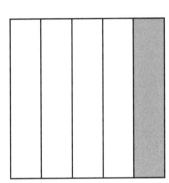

_____

3.

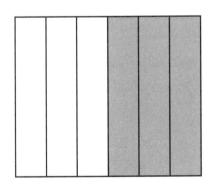

_____

4.

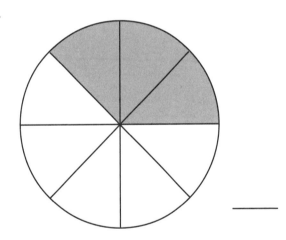

_____

Draw a picture to represent each fraction.

5. $\frac{1}{6}$

6. $\frac{2}{3}$

7. $\frac{3}{5}$

What's a Good Estimate?
Greater Than, Less Than

Build your estimation skills. For each problem, tell if the answer will be less than (<) or greater than (>) the estimate given. Explain why you think so.

1. 7 × 311 is _____ than 2300 because _____

_____

2. 92 ÷ 4 is _____ than 25 because _____

_____

3. $\frac{1}{2}$ of 21 is _____ than 10 because _____

_____

4. 31 ÷ 6 is _____ than 5 because _____

_____

5. $\frac{1}{3}$ of 19 is _____ than 7 because _____

_____

Now, write a problem like one on this page.

_____

▼ **PARENT NOTE:**
Strong estimation skills are important. Estimating before, during, and after calculating the exact answer is one way your child can monitor his or her own thinking.

1

Which Sum Is Greater?

61 + 39 = _____

79 + 21 = _____

Show your thinking.

2

Choose the Answer

Augusto has a plant that grows $2\frac{1}{2}$ in. a week. About how much does it grow in 4 weeks?

A   About 5 in.

B   About $8\frac{1}{2}$ in.

C   About 10 in.

D   About $10\frac{1}{2}$ in.

Explain how you know.

3

Which Is Greater?

Which is greater, $\frac{1}{3}$ of 15 grapes or $\frac{1}{2}$ of 12 grapes?

Show how you know.

4

True or False?

$33 \times 3 \ < \ 32 \times 4$

$45 \times 5 \ < \ 40 \times 10$

$50 \times 2 \ > \ 48 \times 4$

If any statements are false, change them to true statements.

PARENT NOTE:
Problems such as number 3 give students an opportunity to explore the meaning of fractions, and to develop strategies for computing with fractions.

Find the Difference

$9.28
− 6.14

Show your thinking.

Choose the Correct Answer

$65 \div 7 =$ _____

A   7 R6

B   8 R5

C   9 R2

D   10 R5

Explain how you know.

True or False?

$\frac{3}{6} > \frac{6}{8}$

Show how you know.

The Answer Is $\frac{1}{2}$

Write at least 4 different addition and subtraction equations that have this answer.

Solve

$(6 \times 8) \times 2 =$ _____

$6 \times (8 \times 2) =$ _____

Explain your thinking.

Choose the Answer

Which problem has an answer of 6?

A $\frac{1}{2}$ of 24 = _____

B $\frac{1}{3}$ of 12 = _____

C $\frac{1}{6}$ of 36 = _____

D $\frac{1}{5}$ of 25 = _____

Explain how you know.

How Many Feet?

Lila jogged 2 mi. How many feet did she jog?
Hint: 5280 feet = 1 mile

Show your thinking.

True or False?

$75 \div 8 = 9$ R3

Prove it.

Finding Fractions

What fraction of each set of marbles is black?

1. 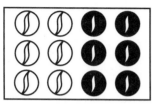 _____

2. 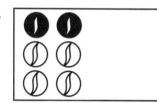 _____

3. 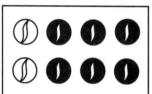 _____

4. 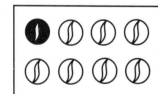 _____

5. 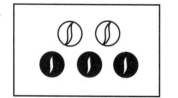 _____

6. _____

7. Pick one set of marbles and explain how you knew what fraction of the set is black.

What's an Easy Way?
Computation Review

Solve these problems as quickly as you can. Use the strategies that work best for you.

Solve.

1. $\frac{1}{2}$ of 4

2. $\frac{1}{4}$ of 12

3. $\frac{1}{2}$ of 6

4. $\frac{1}{5}$ of 10

5. $\frac{1}{3}$ of 9

6. $\frac{1}{2}$ of 40

7. $\frac{1}{4}$ of 20

8. $\frac{1}{3}$ of 15

9. $\frac{1}{5}$ of 25

Write < or > in each ◯ to show which is greater.

10. $\frac{1}{3}$ ◯ $\frac{2}{3}$

11. $\frac{2}{4}$ ◯ $\frac{2}{5}$

12. $\frac{3}{8}$ ◯ $\frac{3}{4}$

13. $\frac{4}{5}$ ◯ $\frac{7}{10}$

14. $\frac{2}{3}$ ◯ $\frac{5}{6}$

15. $\frac{2}{5}$ ◯ $\frac{1}{3}$

Solve.

16. 72 + 96

17. $7.59 + $3.19

18. 67 ÷ 8

19. 15 × 15

20. 182 − 97

Find the Sum

241 + 336 = _____

Explain your thinking.

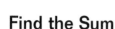

Choose the Answer

7 ft 5 in.
+9 ft 8 in.
_____

A   16 ft 1 in.

B   16 ft 8 in.

C   17 ft

D   17 ft 1 in.

Show your thinking.

True or False?

1200 is a reasonable estimate for
298 × 4

1200 is a reasonable estimate for
478 × 3

1200 is a reasonable estimate for
211 × 6

Can you write a more reasonable
estimate (not exact answer) for
any of these statements?

How Much Money?

A subscription to *Healthy Life*, a
monthly magazine, costs $30 for
1 year. The cover price is $3.
How much money do you save by
getting a 1-year subscription?

Show how you know.

PARENT NOTE:
Addition and subtraction problems involving three-digit numbers, such as number 1, are presented for students to solve using
their own reasoning. Students are presented with appropriate problems and asked to use what they know to find the answers.

Solve

$20 \times 12 =$ _____

Explain your thinking.

Choose the Correct Answer

Which problem has the same answer as $117 + 254 =$ _____ ?

A $145 + 214 =$ _____

B $138 + 233 =$ _____

C $112 + 265 =$ _____

D $173 + 215 =$ _____

Show your thinking.

How Much Money?

Gabrielle has $50.00 to buy new clothes. She buys a pair of shorts for $17.90 and a T-shirt for $12.00. How much money does she have left?

Explain how you know.

The Answer Is 275

Write at least 6 different equations that have this answer.

Solve

$6\overline{)128}$

Explain your thinking.

Choose the Answer

$6.50 + $3.20 = _____

A $8.70

B $9.00

C $9.70

D $9.90

Show your thinking.

True or False?

$\frac{3}{12} = \frac{1}{3}$

Prove it.

Who Paid More?

Lelina paid $10 for a 5-lb bag of granola. Jesse paid $18 for an 8-lb bag of granola. Who paid more money per pound of granola?

Explain how you know.

True or False?

This is how Luis solved the problem:

This square is divided in fourths.
Prove it.

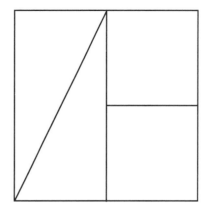

Do you think that Luis proved that the square is divided in fourths?
Explain your thinking.

> **True**
>
> Yes, I think it is
> cut into faurths
> because,
>
> | $\frac{1}{4}$ | $\frac{1}{4}$ |
> |---|---|
> | $\frac{1}{4}$ | $\frac{1}{4}$ |
>
> These
> are thinner
> but longer.
>
> These are
> Shorter but
> fatter.
>
> So they
> are the same.

▼ **PARENT NOTE:**
There are many ways to show fractions. Situations such as this one give students an opportunity to explore dividing a whole into given fractions.

What's Your Strategy?
Convince Me!

Kimi and Bradley's class solved the problem 324 + 485 = _____ . Look at their solutions. Notice that Kimi and Bradley got the same, correct answer, but they used different strategies.

Kimi explained her strategy. The teacher recorded it for the class like this:

Bradley used a different strategy. The teacher recorded his explanation like this:

$$324 + 485 = \underline{\quad}$$

$$500 = 485 + 15$$
$$324 + 500 = 824$$
$$824 - 15 = 809$$

$$324 + 485 = \underline{\quad}$$

$$300 + 400 = 700$$
$$20 + 80 = 100$$
$$4 + 5 = 9$$
$$700 + 100 + 9 = 809$$

Solve the problems below. Record your explanation on paper.

1. 291 + 543

2. 652 + 189

3. 609 + 343

4. 522 + 476

5. 344 + 412

6. 294 + 498

1

Solve

$$\frac{1}{2} + \frac{1}{2} + \frac{1}{4} = \underline{\qquad}$$

Show your thinking.

2

Choose the Correct Answer

Misha started work at 8:30 A.M. Ted started 1 h 20 min earlier. What time did Ted start work?

A   6:50 A.M.

B   7:00 A.M.

C   7:10 A.M.

D   7:30 A.M.

Explain how you know.

3

What Fraction?

Kenji made a pizza. He ate $\frac{1}{3}$ of the pizza and gave $\frac{1}{6}$ to his sister. What fraction of the pizza was left?

Show how you know.

4

Agree or Disagree?

$6.82 + $3.53 = \underline{\qquad}$

Marcia says that the answer is greater than $10.00. Do you agree or disagree?

Explain your thinking.

1

Add

9985 + 15 = _____

Explain your thinking.

2

Which Is False?

A $\frac{1}{4} + \frac{1}{4} = \frac{1}{2}$

B $\frac{1}{2} - \frac{1}{4} = \frac{1}{4}$

C $\frac{3}{4} + \frac{1}{2} = 1\frac{1}{4}$

D $1\frac{1}{2} - \frac{1}{2} = \frac{1}{2}$

Show how you know.

3

What Is Your Story?

Write a story problem for 6 × 18. Show your solution.

4

The Answer Is 1500

Write at least 6 different equations that have this answer.

▼ **PARENT NOTE:**
Problems such as number 3 give students an opportunity to practice a different kind of thinking . To write a story problem, students need to know how all the elements of the problem relate to each other.

Subtract

$$2\frac{3}{4} - \frac{2}{4} = \underline{\hspace{1cm}}$$

Show your thinking.

Choose the Answer

Which problem has a difference of 200?

A $448 - 348 = \underline{\hspace{1cm}}$

B $865 - 565 = \underline{\hspace{1cm}}$

C $723 - 523 = \underline{\hspace{1cm}}$

D $954 - 654 = \underline{\hspace{1cm}}$

Explain how you know.

What Fraction?

Dion's birthday cake was cut into 10 equal slices. Dion ate 2 slices of the cake. What fraction of the cake did he eat? What fraction was left?

Show how you know.

True or False?

360 min = 6 h

120 min = 2 h

3600 min = 6 h

If any statements are false, change them to true statements.

PARENT NOTE:
Problems such as number 4 give students an opportunity to develop their understanding of patterns, and to use these patterns to understand the relationships between different units of measure.

Equivalent Fraction Search

Circle 3 fractions in a row, a column, or a diagonal that are equivalent.
There are 15 sets of equivalent fractions. Can you find them all?

$\dfrac{1}{8}$	$\dfrac{1}{2}$	$\dfrac{3}{6}$	$\dfrac{6}{12}$	$\dfrac{1}{3}$	$\dfrac{1}{5}$
$\dfrac{1}{2}$	$\dfrac{2}{4}$	$\dfrac{3}{6}$	$\dfrac{2}{6}$	$\dfrac{3}{9}$	$\dfrac{1}{3}$
$\dfrac{1}{4}$	$\dfrac{4}{8}$	$\dfrac{3}{9}$	$\dfrac{1}{3}$	$\dfrac{4}{12}$	$\dfrac{5}{6}$
$\dfrac{2}{8}$	$\dfrac{5}{10}$	$\dfrac{3}{4}$	$\dfrac{2}{3}$	$\dfrac{8}{12}$	$\dfrac{6}{9}$
$\dfrac{3}{12}$	$\dfrac{6}{8}$	$\dfrac{4}{6}$	$\dfrac{9}{12}$	$\dfrac{2}{10}$	$\dfrac{4}{6}$
$\dfrac{9}{12}$	$\dfrac{6}{9}$	$\dfrac{5}{12}$	$\dfrac{1}{5}$	$\dfrac{6}{8}$	$\dfrac{2}{3}$

What's a Good Estimate?
It's Between ...

Build your estimation skills. For each problem, write two numbers, one number that is greater than and one number that is less than the exact answer would be. Explain why you chose those numbers.

1325 + 298	78 × 12

_____ and _____   _____ and _____

Why? _____   Why? _____

_____   _____

$7.89 + $4.53 = _____ $61 \div 3 =$ _____

_____ and _____   _____ and _____

Why? _____   Why? _____

_____   _____

Robert brings 8 boxes of old records to the flea market. There are 28 records per box. How many records does Robert bring?

Robert brings between _____ and _____ records.

Why? _____

_____

1

Multiply

$$230 \times 3$$

$$120 \times 4$$

$$310 \times 2$$

Explain your thinking.

2

Choose the Answer

6) 6000

A   10

B   100

C   600

D   1000

Explain how you know.

3

How Many Apples?

Jamal has 15 thirds of apples. How many whole apples does he have?

Show your thinking.

4

True or False?

$$\frac{3}{4} + \frac{2}{4} = 1\frac{1}{2}$$

$$\frac{4}{4} + \frac{2}{4} = 1\frac{1}{2}$$

$$\frac{3}{4} + \frac{3}{4} = 1\frac{1}{2}$$

Did you use one solution to help you find the others? If so, how?

Name _____

Write the Answer

12,000 − 5 = _____

Explain your thinking.

Choose the Answer

At Pizza Barn, pizza is sold by the slice. An eighth of a pizza costs $1.25. Shamika bought $\frac{3}{8}$ of a pizza. How much money did she spend?

A $2.50   C $3.75

B $3.25   D $4.00

Explain how you know.

How Many Cups?

Yoko is tripling a recipe that calls for $\frac{3}{4}$ c of flour. How many cups of flour will Yoko need?

Show your thinking.

The Answer Is $\frac{1}{4}$

Write at least 4 different equations that have this answer. Write both addition and subtraction equations.

PARENT NOTE:
Problems like number 3 give your child practice using math in everyday situations. When possible, ask your child to calculate recipe changes for you.

Name _____

Solve

$8642 \div 2 =$ _____

Explain your thinking.

2

Choose the Best Estimate

$589 - 448 =$ _____

A   About 100

B   About 140

C   About 160

D   About 200

Explain how you know.

True or False?

$\frac{3}{4} - \frac{3}{6} = \frac{1}{2}$

Prove it.

How Many Pizzas?

Tika has 12 half pizzas. How many whole pizzas does she have?

Show your thinking.

▼**PARENT NOTE:**
Multiplication and division problems involving numbers with 2 or more digits, such as number 1, are presented for students to solve using their own reasoning. Students are presented with appropriate problems and asked to use what they know to find the answers.

Name _____

More Cookies!

Change this recipe so it will make 4 dozen cookies.
Show your thinking.

CHOCOLATE CHIP COOKIES

2 eggs

$1\frac{3}{4}$ cup flour

$\frac{1}{2}$ cup butter

1 teaspoon baking soda

$\frac{3}{4}$ cup sugar

$\frac{1}{8}$ teaspoon salt

$\frac{2}{3}$ cup brown sugar

1 six-oz bag of chocolate chips

1 teaspoon vanilla

Bake at 350° for 10–12 minutes.

Makes 2 dozen delicious cookies!

What's an Easy Way?
Computation Review

Solve these problems as quickly as you can. Use the strategies that work best for you.

Solve.

1. $\dfrac{1}{2} + \dfrac{1}{4}$

2. $\dfrac{3}{8} + \dfrac{1}{8}$

3. $\dfrac{1}{4} + \dfrac{3}{4}$

4. $\dfrac{1}{3} + \dfrac{1}{3}$

5. $\dfrac{5}{8} + \dfrac{4}{8}$

6. $\dfrac{2}{9} + \dfrac{5}{9}$

7. $\dfrac{3}{8} + \dfrac{1}{8} + \dfrac{1}{2}$

8. $\dfrac{1}{6} + \dfrac{1}{3} + \dfrac{2}{3}$

9. $\dfrac{1}{2} + \dfrac{2}{3} + \dfrac{1}{2}$

Solve.

10. 5×19

11. $\$6.54 - \$1.19$

12. $363 + 498$

13. 23×12

14. $145 \div 6$

15. $\$7.09 + \$1.99$

16. $1015 + 2902$

17. 7×309

18. $47 \div 6$

19. $\$5.29 - \$3.64$

20. $87 \div 6$

What's the Fraction?

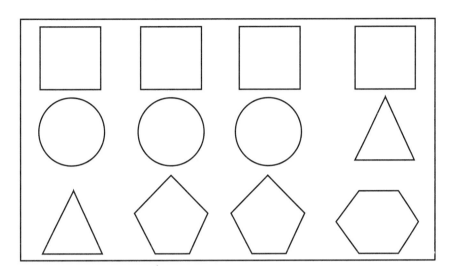

Use the picture to answer the questions. Fill in the bubble next to the correct answer.

1. What fraction shows the part of the set that is ☐s?

- ○ **A.** $\frac{2}{12}$
- ○ **C.** $\frac{3}{12}$
- ○ **B.** $\frac{4}{12}$
- ○ **D.** $\frac{6}{12}$

2. What is another way to show the fraction of the set that is ☐s?

- ○ **A.** $\frac{1}{12}$
- ○ **C.** $\frac{1}{6}$
- ○ **B.** $\frac{1}{4}$
- ○ **D.** $\frac{1}{3}$

3. What fraction shows the part of the set that you have if you count ☐s and ⬠s?

- ○ **A.** $\frac{1}{6}$
- ○ **C.** $\frac{1}{3}$
- ○ **B.** $\frac{1}{2}$
- ○ **D.** $\frac{2}{3}$

4. What is the name of this shape? △

- ○ **A.** circle
- ○ **C.** triangle
- ○ **B.** square
- ○ **D.** pentagon

5. Suppose you compare the ◯s and ⬠s to find which is the greater fraction of the set. Which describes what you find?

- ○ **A.** $\frac{1}{3} > \frac{1}{4}$
- ○ **C.** $\frac{1}{4} > \frac{1}{6}$
- ○ **B.** $\frac{1}{4} > \frac{1}{12}$
- ○ **D.** $\frac{1}{4} < \frac{1}{3}$

What's the Fraction?

The Kaminsky brothers keep track of the time they spend doing homework, and the time they spend reading on their own. The chart below shows their totals for Wednesday.

Name	Time Spent Doing Homework	Time Spent Reading on Their Own
Homer	$1\frac{1}{3}$ hours	$\frac{3}{4}$ hour
Wes	$\frac{2}{3}$ hour	$1\frac{1}{4}$ hours
Paul	$\frac{5}{6}$ hour	1 hour

1. List the names in order from the brother who spent the least time doing homework to the brother who spent the most time doing homework?

2. Who spent the most time reading on his own? Who spent the least? What was the difference in time?

3. Who spent the least total amount of time doing homework and reading? What was that total?

4. How much more time would Paul have to spend doing homework to match Homer?

5. Suppose you wanted to find the number of minutes Paul spent doing homework. How could you do this?

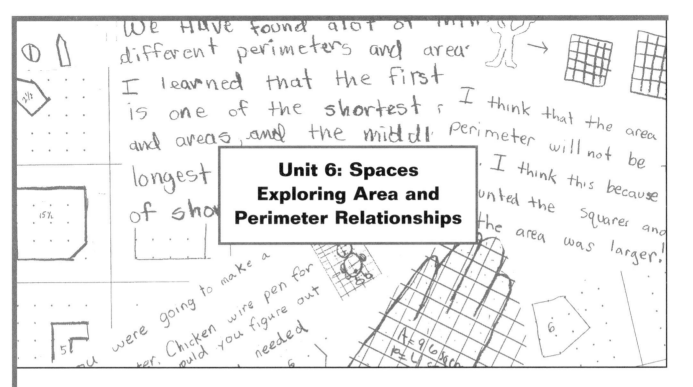

**Unit 6: Spaces
Exploring Area and
Perimeter Relationships**

Thinking Questions

How many different shapes on a geoboard can have an area of 4
square units? Can two shapes have the same perimeter but different
areas? If you had only a certain amount of fencing, how could you
maximize the area that you are to fence in? How could you estimate
the area of an irregular figure such as your hand or foot?

Investigations

In this MathLand unit, you will investigate the relationship between
area and perimeter. Using geoboards and rubber bands, you will learn
what happens to perimeter when you change area and what happens
to area when you change perimeter. You will use these discoveries to
figure out how to estimate the areas of oddly-shaped objects.

Real-World Math

A good understanding of area and perimeter can be very useful in
everyday life. Your class might use these new skills to figure out the
best way to arrange the desks and tables in your classroom. When
was the last time you used area and perimeter?

Math Vocabulary

During this MathLand unit, you may be using some of these words as you talk and write about measurement.

The **perimeter** is the measure around the sides of a polygon.

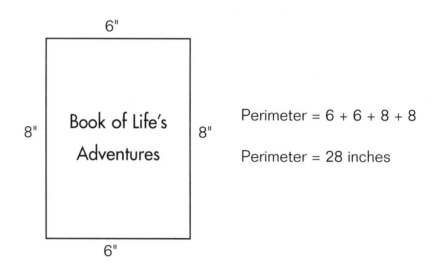

Perimeter = 6 + 6 + 8 + 8

Perimeter = 28 inches

Area is the space inside a shape. Area is measured in square units, such as square inches or square meters.

Area = 4 × 4

Area = 16 square centimeters

A **centimeter** is a unit of measurement in the metric system. There are 100 centimeters in 1 **meter**.

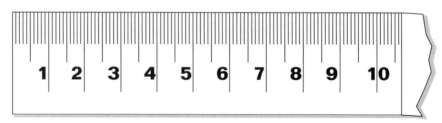

Area or Perimeter?

Read each description in the box. If perimeter is described, color it red. If area is described, color it yellow.

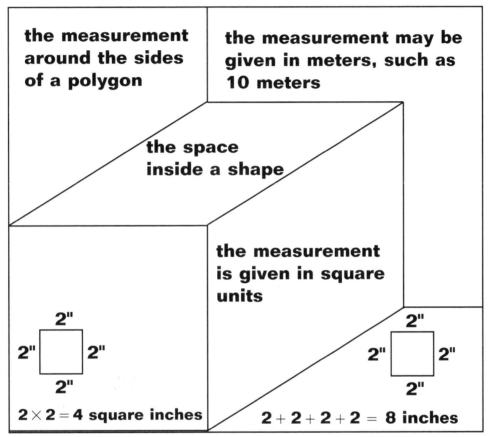

the measurement around the sides of a polygon

the measurement may be given in meters, such as 10 meters

the space inside a shape

the measurement is given in square units

2"
2" □ 2"
2"
$2 \times 2 = 4$ square inches

2"
2" □ 2"
2"
$2 + 2 + 2 + 2 = 8$ inches

Use the centimeter ruler to find items with perimeters of 15 cm and 25 cm.

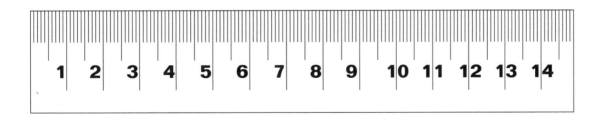

Why did the rectangle talk about his perimeter at the party?

He did not want others to think he was square.

Name _____

1

Write the Answers

186 + 74 = _____

190 + 70= _____

157 + 34 = _____

160 + 31 = _____

What can you say about each pair of equations?
Write another pair of equations like the pair above.

2

Choose the Answer

$8.56
− 3.25
_____

A $4.69

B $5.31

C $5.71

D $5.81

Explain how you know.

3

How Many Yards?

Farid needs 66 ft of string for his science project. How many yards of string does Farid need?

Show your thinking.

4

True or False?

The next number in this pattern is 128.

8, 16, 32, 64, _____

Show how you know.

PARENT NOTE:
Throughout *Skill Power*, pairs of problems such as those in number 1 are presented so that students can develop the technique of using related problems to compute mentally.

1

Solve

350
− 75

Explain your thinking.

2

Choose the Correct Answer

20 + 40 + 60 + 80 = _____

A   160

B   180

C   200

D   220

Show your thinking.

3

Which Is Greater?

Put < or > in each circle to show which is greater.

$\frac{1}{3}$ of 12 ◯ $\frac{1}{4}$ of 12

$\frac{1}{6}$ of 18 ◯ $\frac{1}{2}$ of 18

$\frac{1}{5}$ of 30 ◯ $\frac{1}{6}$ of 30

4

The Answer Is 36

Write at least 6 different equations that have this answer.

Name _____

Write the Answer

4 × 500 = _____

Explain your thinking.

Choose the Answer

Mrs. Romero has 168 in. of rope. How many feet of rope does she have?

A   10 ft

B   12 ft

C   14 ft

D   15 ft

Show how you know.

How Many Marbles?

Rodney has 8 bags of marbles. Each bag has 25 marbles. How many marbles does Rodney have?

Show your thinking.

True or False?

354 ÷ 7 = 5 R4

35 ÷ 7 = 5

350 ÷ 7 = 50

If any statements are false, change them to true statements.

PARENT NOTE:
When children are able to solve multiplication and division involving multiples of 10 or 100, computation becomes easier.

Are They the Same?

1. Draw a shape on the grid that has an area of 10 sq units.
   Label the shape with its area.

2. Draw a shape on the grid that has a perimeter of 10 units.
   Label the shape with its perimeter.

3. Are the two shapes the same size?

4. If the shapes are not the same size, which shape is larger?
   Why do you think one shape is larger than the other?

5. Do you think it is possible to draw one shape that has an area
   of 10 sq units and a perimeter of 10 units? Explain your thinking.

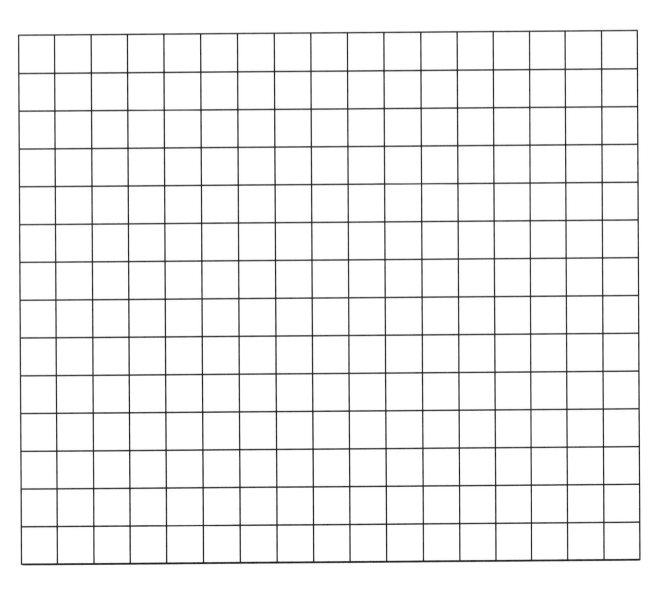

What's a Good Estimate?
Greater Than, Less Than

Build your estimation skills. For each problem, tell if the answer will be less than (<)
or greater than (>) the estimate given. Explain why you think so.

1. 21×53 is _____ than 1000 because _____

_____

2. $379 - 96$ is _____ than 300 because _____

_____

3. $\frac{1}{4}$ of 42 is _____ than 10 because _____

_____

4. 30×47 is _____ than 1500 because _____

_____

5. $80 \div 19$ is _____ than 4 because _____

_____

Now, write a problem like one on this page.

Name _____

© Creative Publications

1

Write the Answers

$6\overline{)44}$ $6\overline{)42}$ $6\overline{)47}$

Show your thinking.

Did you solve one problem first?
Did you use that solution to help
you find the other solutions?
If so, how?

2

Choose the Best Estimate

$121 \times 6 =$ _____

A   About 600

B   About 620

C   About 700

D   About 720

Explain your thinking.

3

How Many Coins?

Marla's coin collection book has
spaces for 18 coins on each
page. There are 10 pages in the
book. She has filled 9 pages. How
many coins are in Marla's book?

Show how you know.

4

True or False?

$\frac{1}{4} + \frac{3}{12} = \frac{1}{2}$

Prove it.

Solve

$936 \div 9 =$ _____

Explain your thinking.

Choose the Answer

Which problem has an answer of 125?

A $6 \times 20 =$ _____

B $12 \times 10 =$ _____

C $5 \times 25 =$ _____

D $6 \times 15 =$ _____

Explain how you know.

How Many Miles?

Eduardo walked $\frac{3}{4}$ mi to school and then $1\frac{1}{4}$ mi to his grandmother's house. How far did Eduardo walk?

Show your thinking.

The Answer Is 50

Write at least 6 different equations that have this answer.

PARENT NOTE:
Problems such as number 3 give students an opportunity to relate measurements and fractions to real-life types of situations.

Write the Answer

4000
×   4

Explain your thinking.

Which Is False?

A $64 \div 8 = 8$

B $56 \div 7 = 8$

C $81 \div 9 = 9$

D $72 \div 9 = 7$

Explain how you know.

How Many Years?

William Wordsworth, an English poet, lived from 1770 until 1850. How many years did he live?

Show your thinking.

True or False?

$312 + 147 < 402 + 88$

Show how you know.

Steven's Shapes

Steven was asked to draw shapes that have a perimeter of 12 cm.

1. Check to see if each of Steven's shapes has a perimeter of 12 cm. Circle any shapes that do not have a perimeter of 12 cm.

2. How many more shapes can you find that have a perimeter of 12 cm? Add your shapes to Steven's grid paper.

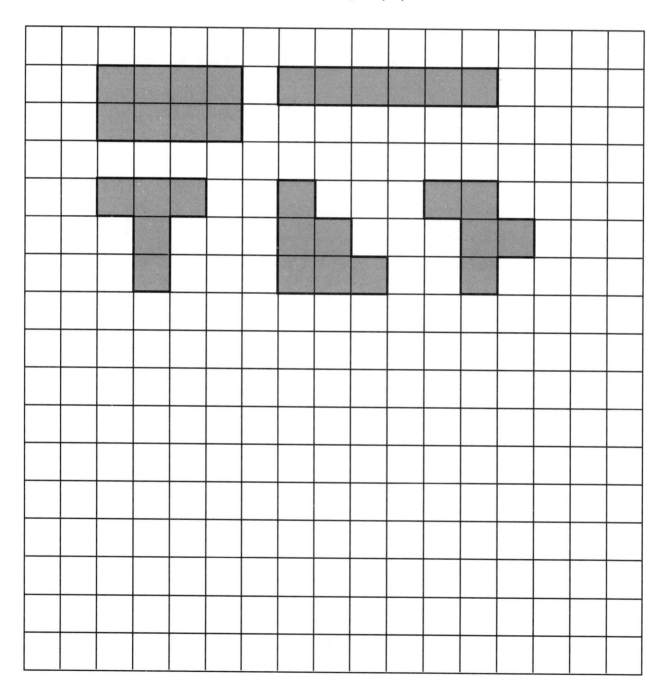

What's an Easy Way?
Computation Review

Solve these problems as quickly as you can. Use the strategies that work best for you.

Solve.

1. 31×9　　　　**2.** $812 + 808$　　　　**3.** 3×4000

4. $756 \div 7$　　　　**5.** $337 - 48$　　　　**6.** 72×14

7. 634×5　　　　**8.** $8000 \div 20$　　　　**9.** 49×20

Write < or > in each ◯ to show which is greater.

10. 23×16 ◯ 25×16　　　　**11.** 4×27 ◯ 5×20

12. $624 \div 4$ ◯ $630 \div 5$　　　　**13.** $93 \div 8$ ◯ $80 \div 5$

Circle the problems that have an answer of 144.

14.　12×12　　　　**15.** 9×15　　　　**16.** $361 - 217$

17.　$576 \div 4$　　　　**18.** $292 \div 3$　　　　**19.** $825 - 671$

20.　$87 + 87$

Solve

$18.26
+ 16.78
───────

Explain your thinking.

Choose the Correct Answer

What is the perimeter of a rectangle that measures 2 cm by 5 cm?

A   7 cm

B   10 cm

C   12 cm

D   14 cm

Explain how you know.

Is There Enough Flour?

Samuel needs $1\frac{1}{2}$ c of flour to make cookies and $2\frac{1}{2}$ c of flour to make bread. There are about $4\frac{1}{4}$ c of flour in the flour jar. Is there enough flour for Samuel to make both the cookies and the bread?

Show your thinking.

Agree or Disagree?

Alma has 6 quarters, 4 dimes, and 3 nickels. She says she has enough money to buy a hamburger for $2.20. Do you agree or disagree?

If you agree, does she have any extra coins? If you disagree, what combination of coins would give her enough money?

▼ PARENT NOTE:
Solving problems such as number 4, for which more than one solution is possible, is an important part of mathematics.

1   Add

$$\begin{array}{r} \frac{3}{9} \\ + \frac{2}{6} \\ \hline \end{array}$$

Explain your thinking.

2   Choose the Correct Answer

Which problem has a quotient that is greater than 10?

A $10\,\overline{)9}$

B $40\,\overline{)200}$

C $20\,\overline{)100}$

D $10\,\overline{)120}$

Explain how you know.

3   True or False?

$\frac{1}{2}$ of 12 = 6

$\frac{1}{3}$ of 12 = 4

$\frac{1}{6}$ of 12 = 10

If any statements are false, write one way to make them true.

4   The Answer Is 200

Write at least 6 different equations that have this answer.

Name _____

Solve

```
  3423
-  241
```

Show your thinking.

2

Choose the Answer

$8\overline{)643}$

A   80 R3

B   83

C   90 R3

D   93

Explain how you know.

How Old Was He?

Franklin Delano Roosevelt was born in 1882. He became president of the United States in 1933. How old was Roosevelt when he became president?

Explain your thinking.

True or False?

$23 \times 6 = 136$

$20 \times 6 = 120$

$3 \times 6 = 18$

What do you notice about these statements?

▼ **PARENT NOTE:**
Students have considerable experience with equal-sharing situations in their daily lives. At school, they can use and build on these experiences as they discuss and solve division situations.

Finding Area and Perimeter

1. Find the area and perimeter of each shape.

2. List the shapes from the least to greatest area.

3. List the shapes from the least to greatest perimeter.

4. Compare the two lists. How do you think area and perimeter are related? Explain your thinking.

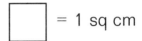 = 1 sq cm

A.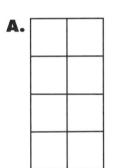

B.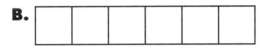

C.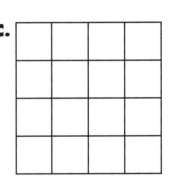

D.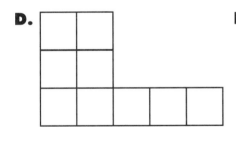

E.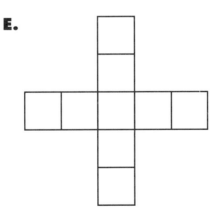

F.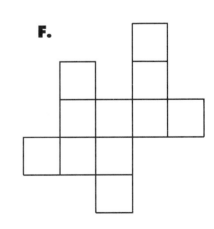

What's Your Strategy?
Convince Me!

Ned and Fran's class solved the problem $1\frac{1}{3} - \frac{5}{6} = $ _____ . Look at their solutions. Notice that Ned and Fran got the same, correct answer, but they used different strategies.

Ned explained his strategy. The teacher recorded it for the class like this:

Fran used a different strategy. The teacher recorded her explanation like this:

$1\frac{1}{3} - \frac{5}{6} = $ _____

$\frac{1}{3} = \frac{2}{6}$, so take $\frac{2}{6}$ from $\frac{5}{6}$
That leaves $\frac{3}{6}$ more to be
subtracted. $\frac{3}{6} = \frac{1}{2}$

$1 - \frac{1}{2} = \frac{1}{2}$

$1\frac{1}{3} - \frac{5}{6} = $ _____

$1\frac{1}{3} = 1\frac{2}{6} = \frac{8}{6}$

$\frac{8}{6} - \frac{5}{6} = \frac{3}{6}$

$\frac{3}{6} = \frac{1}{2}$

Solve the problems below. Record your explanation on paper.

1. $1\frac{1}{4} - \frac{3}{8}$

2. $1\frac{2}{3} - \frac{5}{6}$

3. $1\frac{1}{2} - \frac{7}{8}$

4. $1\frac{1}{3} - \frac{5}{9}$

5. $1\frac{3}{5} - \frac{4}{5}$

6. $1\frac{1}{5} - \frac{7}{10}$

What's the Measurement?

ROOM SIZES IN SAM'S APARTMENT

Bedroom	120 square feet
Living room	200 square feet
Bathroom	70 square feet
Storage room	40 square feet
Kitchen	110 square feet

Fill in the bubble next to the correct answer.

1. Which list shows the rooms from greatest number of square feet to least number of square feet?

○ **A.** Storage room, Bathroom, Bedroom, Kitchen, Living room

○ **B.** Storage room, Bathroom, Kitchen, Bedroom, Living room

○ **C.** Living room, Kitchen, Bedroom, Storage room, Bathroom

○ **D.** Living room, Bedroom, Kitchen, Bathroom, Storage room

2. What is the difference in size between the two smallest rooms?

○ **A.** 10 square feet

○ **B.** 30 square feet

○ **C.** 20 square feet

○ **D.** 40 square feet

3. About how large is the apartment? Choose the best estimate.

○ **A.** 400 square feet

○ **B.** 550 square feet

○ **C.** 500 square feet

○ **D.** 600 square feet

4. The bedroom is 10 feet long and 12 feet wide. What is the perimeter?

○ **A.** 22 feet   ○ **C.** 34 feet

○ **B.** 44 feet   ○ **D.** 56 feet

5. Suppose Sam wants to carpet the bedroom and the living room. Carpet costs $2.79 per square foot. Which gives the closest estimate of the cost?

○ **A.** 300 × $2.00   ○ **C.** 320 × $2.00

○ **B.** 300 × $3.00   ○ **D.** 320 × $3.00

What's the Measurement?

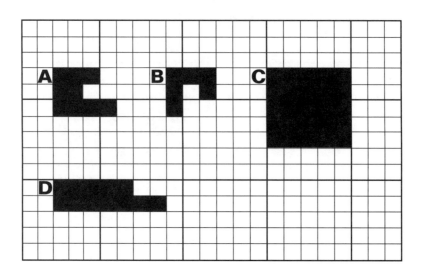

1. List the shapes from greatest area to least area.

2. List the shapes from greatest perimeter to least perimeter.

3. Could you add a square to shape B so that you *decreased* the perimeter? Explain.

4. Suppose you added 1 square to any part of shape C. How would that change the area? How would that change the perimeter?

5. Suppose each square represented a shape that was 5 m on each side. For shape D, what area would the shape represent? What perimeter would it represent?

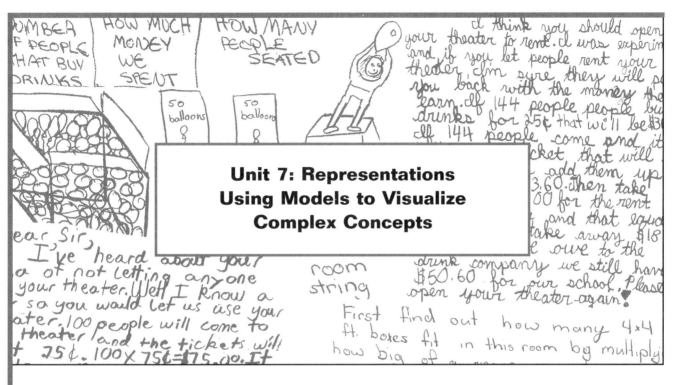

Thinking Questions

What does the number 100 look like? What about 1000? How can you model these numbers with squares or cubes? Can these number models help you to do multiplication and division? What other types of models can you use to figure out prices and profits or estimate how many jelly beans there are in a jar?

Investigations

In this MathLand unit, you will use models to develop your ability to visualize more advanced math concepts. Seeing models of large numbers can help you to discover number patterns and to solve complex problems. By working with these models, you will develop your mental math skills and improve your ability to make accurate estimates.

Real-World Math

Modeling is a technique that can be used in everyday life. Meteorologists use models to help them predict the weather. Economists use models to help them to understand how the economy works. Where have you seen models being used?

Math Vocabulary

During this MathLand unit, you may be using some of these words as you talk and write about complex concepts.

A **solid** is a three dimensional shape.

A **face** of a solid is one of its flat surfaces.

A **cube** is a three-dimensional (3-D) figure that has squares for all of its six faces.

A **rectangular solid** is a three-dimensional (3-D) shape, such as a box, with six rectangular faces.

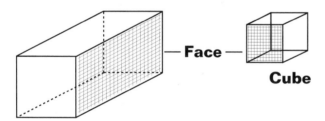

Rectangular solid

A **model** is a copy of something. A model can be bigger, smaller, or the same size as the object.

Example: a model airplane

A **range** is the difference between the greatest measure and the least measure.

Example: Students' guesses for the number of peanuts in a jar ranged from 50 to 695.

To **estimate** is to figure out the approximate amount. In this unit, you will find that estimation is an important technique when working with large numbers.

Example: By quickly counting the people in one section of the arena, he estimated there were about 1000 people at the game.

Visualization is forming a picture in your mind of something. Visualizing smaller groups of numbers can help you make more accurate estimates of large numbers.

Name _____

Clues for You

Read the following clues and write the correct vocabulary word on the blanks. Unscramble the letters in the circles to figure out the riddle.

1. a 3-D solid shape
6 rectangular faces

_ _ _◯_ _ _ _ _ _ _   _◯_ _ _ _

2. difference between measures
greatest and least

_ _◯_ _

3. a copy
bigger, smaller, or the same size

◯◯_ _ _

4. 3-D
square faces

_ _ _◯

5. picture in your mind
for making estimates

_◯_ _ _ _◯_ _◯_ _ _

6. flat surface
on 3-D solids

_◯_ _

Guess what! ◯◯◯◯◯◯◯◯◯ is an important math tool.

1

Write the Answer

$2.30
×   9

Show your thinking.

2

Choose the Answers

Look at the 4 possible answers. Which 2 answers would you rule out first?

$4 \times 79 =$ _____

A   108   C   316

B   166   D   320

Explain your thinking.

3

What Is the Difference?

The area of Massachusetts is 7826 sq mi. The area of Connecticut is 4862 sq mi. How much larger is Massachusetts?

Explain how you know.

4

True or False?

If the numerator of a fraction is greater than the denominator, then the fraction is greater than 1.

Prove it.

▼ **PARENT NOTE:**
Problem number 2 provides students with an opportunity to use estimation to eliminate unreasonable answers, a skill that is useful on multiple-choice tests.

Divide

$$6\overline{)667}$$

Show your thinking.

Choose the Correct Answer

With which 3 numbers can you write a true subtraction equation?

A   85, 65, 20

B   65, 15, 25

C   42, 10, 22

D   8, 26, 17

Show how you know.

What Was the Average?

During their vacation, Felicia and her family drove 52 mi in 2 h. What was the average distance they traveled in an hour?

Explain how you know.

The Answer Is 400

Write at least 6 different equations that have this answer.

Write the Answers

$65 + 25 + 20 =$ _____

$65 + 25 + 23 =$ _____

$68 + 25 + 20 =$ _____

$65 + 28 + 20 =$ _____

Show your thinking.

Choose the Answer

$3\frac{3}{4} + 5\frac{1}{4} =$ _____

A $\quad 8\frac{3}{4}$

B $\quad 8\frac{1}{4}$

C $\quad 9$

D $\quad 9\frac{1}{4}$

Explain how you know.

How Many Meals?

Peter eats 3 meals every day. How many meals does Peter eat in 1 year? How many does he eat in 2 years?

Explain your thinking.

True or False?

A rectangular rabbit enclosure measures 3 ft by 4 ft. True or false? The perimeter is 14 ft.

Show how you know.

Finish the Facts

Use the numbers 2–9 to complete these two multiplication equation puzzles. Use each number only once.

1.
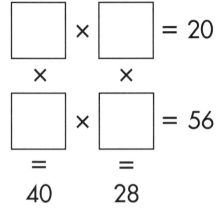

$\square \times \square = 20$

$\times \qquad \times$

$\square \times \square = 56$

$= \qquad =$

40 \qquad 28

2.
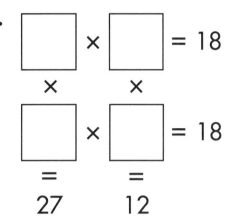

$\square \times \square = 18$

$\times \qquad \times$

$\square \times \square = 18$

$= \qquad =$

27 \qquad 12

Use the numbers 2–9 to complete these two multiplication equation puzzles. Use each number only once.

3.

$\square \times \square = 63$

$\times \qquad \times$

$\square \times \square = 10$

$= \qquad =$

45 \qquad 14

4.

$\square \times \square = 24$

$\times \qquad \times$

$\square \times \square = 24$

$= \qquad =$

48 \qquad 12

5. Create your own multiplication equation puzzle for a friend or family member to solve. Show your solution.

What's a Good Estimate?
It's Between ...

Build your estimation skills. For each problem, write two numbers, one number that is greater than and one number that is less than the exact answer would be. Explain why you chose those numbers.

$$\begin{array}{r} \$4.35 \\ \times \quad 5 \\ \hline \end{array}$$

_____ and _____

Why? _____

_____

$$\begin{array}{r} 2572 \\ + \quad 844 \\ \hline \end{array}$$

_____ and _____

Why? _____

_____

6008 − 654 = _____

_____ and _____

Why? _____

_____

143 ÷ 6 = _____

_____ and _____

Why? _____

_____

Rhea is buying eight tickets for her family and friends. The tickets cost $4.75 each. How much money does Rhea need?

Rhea needs between $ _____ and $ _____

Why? _____

Find the Difference

5000 − 738 = _____

Show your thinking.

Choose the Answer

Fernando averaged 45 mph on an 8-h trip. How many miles did he travel?

A   300 mi

B   360 mi

C   400 mi

D   445 mi

Explain your thinking.

How Many Days?

During the summer, Felipe and his family went camping for 4 weeks. How many days did they go camping?

Show how you know.

Which Is Greater?

Put < or > in each circle to show which is greater.

3 × 8 × 2 ◯ 3 × 9 × 2

4 × 7 × 9 ◯ 4 × 7 × 8

5 × 2 × 6 ◯ 6 × 2 × 6

Show how you know.

Write the Answers

$18 \div 3 =$ _____

$180 \div 3 =$ _____

$180 \div 30 =$ _____

$1800 \div 30 =$ _____

What do you notice about these problems? Write another equation to fit this series.

Choose the Best Estimate

$$\begin{array}{r} 61 \\ \times\ 4 \\ \hline \end{array}$$

Which number is closest to the product?

A   200

B   240

C   260

D   300

Explain how you know.

How Much Money?

Lisa made $24,000 last year. She was paid the same amount each month. How much money did Lisa earn each month?

Show your thinking.

The Answer Is 1000

Write at least 6 different equations that have this answer.

▼PARENT NOTE:
The Answer Is... problems ask students to find several ways to represent the same number. Your child's entries for these problems will give you information about his/her developing number understandings.

Which Is Greater?

6 × 40 = _____

7 × 30 = _____

Explain your thinking.

Choose the Answer

Which problem has a product of $4.90?

A   5 × 95¢ = _____

B   6 × 75¢ = _____

C   7 × 70¢ = _____

D   8 × 50¢ = _____

Explain how you know.

How Many Tens?

If 10 tens equal 100, how many tens equal 1000?

Show your thinking.

True or False?

564 ÷ 7 = 80 R4

Show how you know.

Equations for 100,000

Write 5 different equations that have an answer of 100,000.
Use addition, subtraction, multiplication, and division in
each equation.

Here is an example for 10:

$$(6 \div 2) \times 4 + 9 - 11 = 10$$

1. _____ = 100,000

2. _____ = 100,000

3. _____ = 100,000

4. _____ = 100,000

5. _____ = 100,000

What's an Easy Way?
Computation Review

Solve these problems as quickly as you can. Use the strategies that work best for you.

Solve.

1. 5×78

2. $450 \div 6$

3. 8×93

4. $563 \div 7$

5. 50×12

6. 9×54

7. $900 \div 30$

8. $30 \times 20 \times 10$

9. $620 \div 7$

Write < or > in each $\bigcirc$ to show which is greater.

10. 23×9 $\bigcirc$ 200

11. $623 \div 8$ $\bigcirc$ 80

12. 12×24 $\bigcirc$ 300

13. $164 + 637$ $\bigcirc$ 800

Circle the problems that have an answer of 424.

14. $848 \div 3$

15. 106×4

16. $188 + 236$

17. $2 \times 53 \times 4$

18. 6×41

19. $752 - 328$

20. $212 + 312$

Divide

$13 \overline{)104}$

Explain your thinking.

Choose the Correct Answer

Bill saw a movie that began at 7:15 P.M. and ended at 9:35 P.M. How long was the movie?

A   2 h 5 min

B   2 h 15 min

C   2 h 20 min

D   2 h 25 min

Explain how you know.

True or False?

The next number in this pattern is 44.

9, 18, 27, 36, _____

Show how you know.

How Many Blocks?

There are 6 rows of 15 blocks. How many blocks are there in all?

Show your thinking.

1

Find the Products

15 × 10 = _____

15 × 12 = _____

Explain your thinking.

2

Choose the Answer

Which problem has a difference of 8?

A   90 − 82 = _____

B   68 − 59 = _____

C   75 − 61 = _____

D   57 − 48 = _____

Explain how you know.

3

True or False?

If any statements are false, make them true.

One third is equivalent to $\frac{2}{6}$ and to $\frac{3}{9}$.

One half is equivalent to $\frac{2}{3}$ and to $\frac{4}{6}$.

One fourth is equivalent to $\frac{2}{8}$ and to $\frac{3}{12}$.

Explain your thinking.

4

The Answer Is 193

Write at least 6 different equations that have this answer.

Multiply

38
× 20

Explain your thinking.

Choose the Answer

Joslyn bought 6 boxes of her favorite cereal for $3.19 each. How much money did Joslyn spend for cereal?

A $18.76   C $19.20

B $19.14   D $20.19

Explain how you know.

How Old Was He?

Martin Luther King, Jr., was born in 1929. In 1964 he was awarded the Nobel Peace Prize. How old was King when he received the Nobel Peace Prize?

Show your thinking.

True or False?

300 is a reasonable estimate for 19 × 15.

300 is a reasonable estimate for 18 × 24.

300 is a reasonable estimate for 11 × 25.

Explain how you know.
Can you write a more reasonable estimate (not exact answer) for any of these statements?

▼ **PARENT NOTE:**
Try estimating some answers yourself and noticing the different ways you approach problems.

Find the Product

This is how Leslie solved the problem:

27 × 13 = _____

Do you agree or disagree with her work?
Explain your thinking.

$$
\begin{array}{r}
27 \\
\times\ 1\,3 \to 10 \\
\hline
\end{array}
$$

$$
\begin{array}{r}
27 \\
\times\ 1\,0 \\
\hline
270
\end{array}
+
\begin{array}{r}
3 \\
\times\ 27 \\
\hline
81
\end{array}
= 351
$$

I did it by rounding 13 to 10. Then I multiplied 27 and 10 together and got 270. I got that because whenever you multiply a number by 10 you just add a zero. Next I did 3 × 27. I did that by doing 3 × 20 then 3 × 7 and adding those I got 81. Last I added 270 and 81 and got 351.

What's Your Strategy?
Convince Me!

Ruben and Sarah's class solved the problem 22 × 38 = _____ . Look at their solutions. Notice that Ruben and Sarah got the same, correct answer, but they used different strategies.

Ruben explained his strategy. The teacher recorded it for the class like this:

22 x 38 = _____

20 x 38 = 760

2 x 38 = 76

760 + 76 = 836

Sarah used a different strategy. The teacher recorded her explanation like this:

22 x 38 = _____

20 x 30 = 600

20 x 8 = 160

2 x 30 = 60

2 x 8 = 16

600 + 160 + 60 + 16 = 836

Solve the problems below. Record your explanation on paper.

1. 27 × 35

2. 13 × 18

3. 19 × 32

4. 53 × 12

5. 32 × 31

6. 23 × 29

Write the Answer

$(4 \times 6) \times 6 =$ _____

Show your thinking.

Choose the Correct Answer

How many cans of soda are there in 23 six-packs of soda?

A   92 cans

B   120 cans

C   136 cans

D   138 cans

Explain how you know.

How Long Did It Last?

World War II began in 1939 and ended in 1945. How many years did World War II last?

Show how you know.

Agree or Disagree?

Sun-Lee got an answer of 550 for this problem. Do you agree or disagree with Sun-Lee's answer?

```
  586
+  74
```

Explain your thinking.

1

Find the Product

25
×12

Show your thinking.

2

Choose the Answer

On Saturday Wes and Damon sold lemonade at the corner near their school. They spent $18.65 on lemonade and cups. At the end of the day, they had $33.17. What was their profit?

A $13.48   C $15.48

B $14.52   D $51.82

Explain how you know.

3

What Was the Total?

At the local movie theater, tickets are $6.25. A small popcorn is $2.50 and a small soda is $1.50. Rita took her 2 friends to see *Dinosaur Mystery*. Each of the 3 girls bought a box of popcorn and a soda. How much did they spend all together?

Explain your thinking.

4

The Answer Is $1

Write at least 6 different equations that have this answer.

Subtract

683
− 149

Show your thinking.

Choose the Correct Answer

Which problem has an answer greater than 100?

A $(3 \times 7) \times 3 =$ _____

B $(5 \times 8) \times 2 =$ _____

C $(7 \times 5) \times 3 =$ _____

D $(6 \times 8) \times 2 =$ _____

Show your thinking.

How Many Tickets?

Ruben and Jean were in charge of the Ball Toss game at their school fair. The price per ticket was $0.50. How many tickets did Ruben and Jean need to sell to make their goal of $45.00?

Explain how you know.

True or False?

Thirty-two cents is $\frac{1}{4}$ of $1.28.

Explain your thinking.

Food at the Park

Alice, Delia, Gwen, and Sara went to the park. Each girl had $10.00. They each bought a ride ticket and something to eat. No girl went on the same ride as any of the others. What did each girl buy to eat?

Ferris Wheel	Merry-Go-Round
$3.50	$2.00

Pony Ride	Train Ride
$2.50	$3.75

Soda	Ice Cream	Fruit Bar
$1.00	$2.10	$1.75

Change each girl got:

Alice	$5.75
Delia	$5.90
Gwen	$4.50
Sara	$4.40

1. Alice _____

2. Delia _____

3. Gwen _____

4. Sara _____

▼PARENT NOTE:
Pay close attention to your child's thinking about a problem, not just the answer. Learning how to approach problems is a valuable life-long skill.

Name _____

What's a Good Estimate?
Greater Than, Less Than

Build your estimation skills. For each problem, tell if the answer will be less than (<) or greater than (>) the estimate given. Explain why you think so.

1. 16 x 41 is _____ than 500 because _____

_____

2. 29 x 27 is _____ than 900 because _____

_____

3. 225 ÷ 24 is _____ than 10 because _____

_____

4. 557 ÷ 8 is _____ than 70 because _____

_____

5. 49 x 12 is _____ than 525 because _____

_____

Now, write a problem like one on this page.

Find the Product

99
× 9

Explain your thinking.

Choose the Answer

The 49ers won their game by over 20 points. The Falcons scored 13 points. Which of the following could be the 49ers' score?

A   20 points   C   30 points

B   25 points   D   35 points

Explain how you know.

How Many Years?

The first moon landing by humans was achieved by Apollo II in 1969. How many years has it been since the first moon landing?

Show your thinking.

True or False?

300 is a reasonable estimate for 842 – 639.

300 is a reasonable estimate for 784 – 476.

300 is a reasonable estimate for 673 – 295.

Can you write a more reasonable estimate (not exact answer) for any of these statements?

Name _____

Find the Sum

999 + 999 = _____

Explain your thinking.

Choose the Answer

Rob bought four $20-shirts at a "2 for 1" sale. How much money did he pay for the 4 shirts?

A $10

B $20

C $40

D $80

Explain how you know.

How Many Pennies?

Shayne had 9 quarters, 23 dimes, and 10 nickels. She changed all of her money into pennies. How many pennies did she have?

Show your thinking.

The Answer Is 500

Write at least 4 different multiplication equations that have this answer.

PARENT NOTE:
To solve addition and subtraction problems, such as number 1, a student may use a few strategies over and over. Students add new strategies gradually, as their thinking and number sense develop.

Write the Answers

$9\overline{)99}$ $9\overline{)101}$ $9\overline{)96}$

Explain your thinking.

Choose the Correct Answer

One bean weighs 4 g. About how many beans are there in a bag of beans that weighs 429 g?

A   About 47 beans

B   About 93 beans

C   About 107 beans

D   About 407 beans

Explain how you know.

How Much Is the Fine?

The speed limit is 55 mph. Nicole got a ticket for going 70 mph. Suppose the fine is $10 per mile over the speed limit. How much money is Nicole's fine?

Show your thinking.

True or False?

1 dime = $\frac{1}{10}$ of a dollar.

2 dimes = $\frac{1}{5}$ of a dollar.

4 dimes = $\frac{4}{5}$ of a dollar.

Show how you know.

PARENT NOTE:
Problems such as number 4 help students relate different methods of expressing a money amount, such as combinations of coins and fractions of a dollar. Expressing amounts in different ways helps students build their number sense and understanding of equivalencies.

How Many Are There?

Count the number of items in each square. Estimate the total
number of items there would be for the given number of squares.

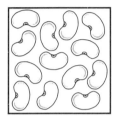

	Number of Squares	Estimated Total Number of Beans
1.	35	_____
2.	617	_____
3.	149	_____

	Number of Squares	Estimated Total Number of Rice Grains
4.	57	_____
5.	432	_____
6.	687	_____

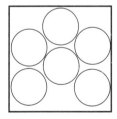

	Number of Squares	Estimated Total Number of Candies
7.	86	_____
8.	873	_____
9.	263	_____

10. Explain how you estimated your answers.

What's an Easy Way?
Computation Review

Solve these problems as quickly as you can. Use the strategies that work best for you.

Solve.

1. 12×16 **2.** 32×20 **3.** $240 \div 12$

4. 21×15 **5.** $496 \div 16$ **6.** 25×25

7. $430 \div 20$ **8.** 42×23 **9.** $257 \div 16$

What number multiplied by itself gives the product? Use the same number to fill in both blanks.

10. $9 =$ _____ $\times$ _____   **11.** $900 =$ _____ $\times$ _____

12. $121 =$ _____ $\times$ _____   **13.** $400 =$ _____ $\times$ _____

Solve.

14. $325 - 168$ **15.** $488 + 999$ **16.** $76 \div 5$

17. 6×808 **18.** $724 \div 8$ **19.** $1200 + 3702$

20. 9×611

What's the Profit?

Name of Item	Jayne's Cost	Jayne's Price	Profit Per 1 Item (Price-Cost)	Number of Items Sold This Week
Brass Deer	$1.50	$3.19		28
Card Collection	$0.62	$1.29		41
Souvenir Pen	$1.00	$2.79		56
Snow Bubble	$0.60	$1.49		25

Jayne runs a souvenir shop. The table gives information about some items that she sells. Jayne has not yet completed the third column of the table. You can fill it in to help you answer the questions.

Fill in the bubble next to the correct answer.

1. Which item gives the greatest profit per 1 item?

○ **A.** brass deer

○ **B.** souvenir pen

○ **C.** card collection

○ **D.** snow bubble

2. About how much greater is the profit on one souvenir pen than the profit on one card collection? Round to the nearest 10 cents.

○ **A.** $0.70 ○ **C.** $1.10

○ **B.** $1.20 ○ **D.** $1.80

3. How much profit in all does Jayne make from the snow bubbles that she sold this week?

○ **A.** $17.80 ○ **C.** $22.25

○ **B.** $ 37.25 ○ **D.** $47.32

4. Which is the closest estimate of Jayne's profit from the souvenir pens this week?

○ **A.** more than $50

○ **B.** between $100 and $120

○ **C.** between $75 and $100

○ **D.** more than $120

5. Suppose Jayne sells 43 brass deer one week. Which gives the closest estimate of the total that customers pay for the deer?

○ **A.** 40 × $3.00 ○ **C.** 50 × $3.00

○ **B.** 40 × $4.00 ○ **D.** 50 × $4.00

What Does the Picture Show?

Martin sells bags of marbles.

1. Suppose there are the same number of marbles in each bag. How many marbles are in 39 bags?

2. The same combination of marbles is in each bag. What number sentence would you use to find out the number of striped marbles in 45 bags?

3. Martin has 2448 marbles. What number sentence would you use to find how many bags Martin can fill?

4. What fraction of the marbles is white?

5. Suppose you closed your eyes and picked a marble. Which kind of marble would you be most likely to pick? Which kind of marble would you be least likely to pick?

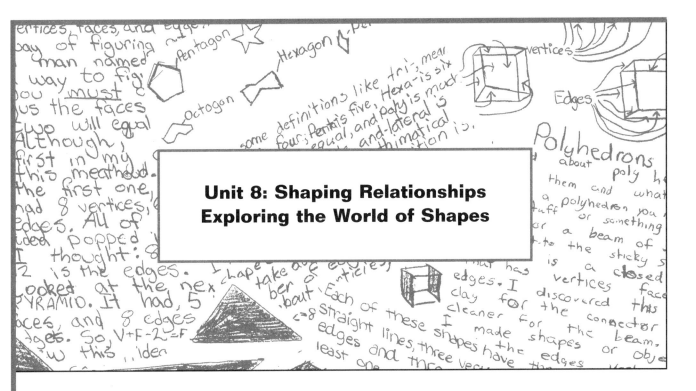

Unit 8: Shaping Relationships
Exploring the World of Shapes

Thinking Questions

What kinds of shapes can you make using construction paper? What kind of shape puzzles can you make using tangrams or Polygon Tiles? What are the similarities and differences among all of the shapes that you have made? Can you sort them into groups? Can you construct and analyze more complex shapes?

Investigations

This MathLand unit lets you examine the world of shapes: how to build them, how to classify them, and how to discover the mathematical patterns within them. You will build two-dimensional and three-dimensional shapes, and you will discover ways to sort them into groups. You will develop your spatial and logical thinking skills by investigating the mathematical relationships that exist in complex shapes.

Real-World Math

You see shapes everywhere in the world: in buildings, in art, in your classroom, and in your kitchen. Is there one particular shape that you see time and time again?

Math Vocabulary

During this MathLand unit, you may be using some of these words as you talk and write about geometry.

When a figure is folded along a **line of symmetry**, each side is a mirror image of the other side. A figure may have more than one line of symmetry.

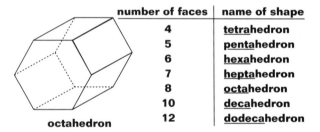

A **polyhedron** is a solid figure with 4 or more faces that are polygons. Polyhedrons are named according to the number of faces they have.

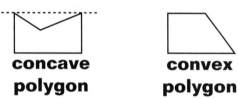

number of faces	name of shape
4	tetrahedron
5	pentahedron
6	hexahedron
7	heptahedron
8	octahedron
10	decahedron
12	dodecahedron

octahedron

Tessellating means covering a space completely with repetitions of one shape or a combination of shapes.

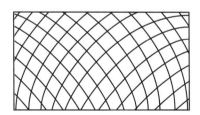

A **concave polygon** is a polygon that looks "caved in." Two vertices of a concave polygon can be connected by a line outside the polygon. Two vertices of a **convex polygon** cannot be connected outside the polygon.

concave polygon   **convex polygon**

All polyhedrons have vertices, edges, and faces. A **vertex** is a corner. It is where two or more lines intersect. An **edge** is a line that connects two vertices. A **face** is one surface of a solid figure.

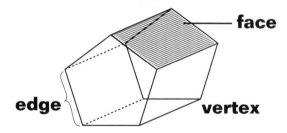

Euler was a great mathematician who lived more than 200 years ago. He proved a relationship that is true for all polyhedrons. You will learn about **Euler's Theorem** in this unit.

Geometry Crossword

Use the clues and the words in the word bank to solve the word puzzle.

Word Bank

concave
convex
edges
equilateral
Euler
faces
hexomino
parallelogram
polyhedron
symmetry
tessellating
Theorem
vertices

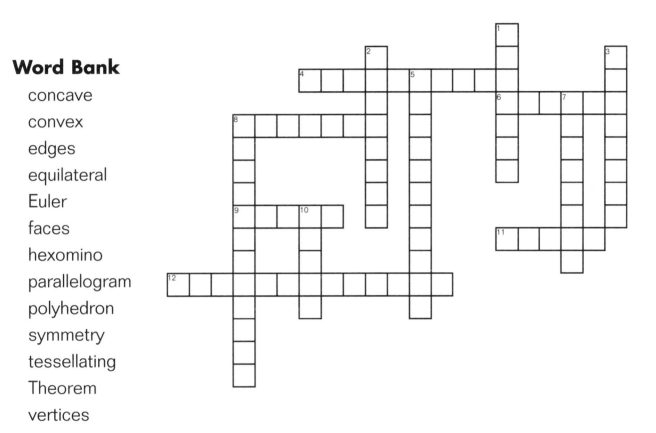

Across

4. solid figure with 4 or more polygon faces
6. 2 of its vertices can't be connected
8. Euler's _____
9. a mathematician
11. surfaces of a solid figure
12. ▱

Down

1. looks "caved in"
2. 2 sides are mirror images of each other
3. flat surface made with 6 squares
5. triangle with 3 sides of equal length
7. corners
8. the repeating of 1 shape
10. lines connecting 2 or more vertices

Name _____

Find the Difference

$12.76 – $8.42 = _____

Show your thinking.

Choose the Answer

What is the area of a rectangle that is 7 cm long and 6 cm wide?

A   13 sq cm

B   26 sq cm

C   42 sq cm

D   52 sq cm

Show how you know.

How Much Money?

Eddie had $20.00. He bought a science experiment kit for $12.73. How much money does he have left over?

Explain your thinking.

True or False?

The sum of 28 + 74 is greater than the sum of 35 + 59.

Explain how you know.

Find the Sum

1345 + 995 = _____

Explain your thinking.

Choose the Answer

Which problem has a product of 500?

A   20 × 50 = _____

B   6 × 75 = _____

C   10 × 50 = _____

D   11 × 48 = _____

Explain how you know.

True or False?

You can write a true equation with these 3 numbers.

8, 9, 57

Prove it.

The Answer Is 5000

Write at least 6 different equations that have this answer.

1

Solve

26	17	34
× 9	× 9	× 9

Explain your thinking.

2

Choose the Correct Answer

16 × 17 = _____

A   72

B   172

C   272

D   2072

Explain how you know.

3

How Many Eat Fruit?

Jerome surveyed 100 people about their eating habits. Four fifths of the people surveyed said that they ate fruit regularly. How many people surveyed eat fruit regularly?

Show your thinking.

4

True or False?

10 × $18.08 > $180.08

100 × $1.08 < $1080.00

10 × $1.08 < $18.00

Tell how you know.

Friendly Fred's Floor Company

Friendly Fred's Floor Company puts in tile floors. This is a picture of the most popular arrangement of tiles.

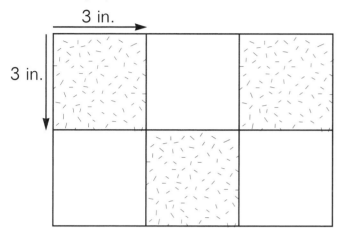

How many dotted tiles should Fred order for the following areas?

1. 9 in. by 12 in. area _____

2. 18 in. by 12 in. area _____

3. 9 in. by 18 in. area _____

4. 18 in. by 24 in. area _____

Fred ordered the following numbers of dotted tiles. What are the dimensions of the area that will fit tiles in this pattern?

5. 8 dotted tiles _____

6. 12 dotted tiles _____

7. 10 dotted tiles _____

8. 18 dotted tiles _____

▼ **PARENT NOTE:**
Solving problems such as numbers 5–8, for which more than one solution is possible, is an important part of mathematics.

What's a Good Estimate?
It's Between ...

Build your estimation skills. For each problem, write two numbers, one number that is greater than and one number that is less than the exact answer would be. Explain why you chose those numbers.

$$39 \times 12$$

_____ and _____

Why? _____

_____

$$7287 + 1348$$

_____ and _____

Why? _____

_____

$$\$12.58 - \$9.69 = \underline{\hspace{1cm}}$$

_____ and _____

Why? _____

_____

$$260 \div 25 = \underline{\hspace{1cm}}$$

_____ and _____

Why? _____

_____

George is collecting stamps. He already has 379 stamps. A book holds 750 stamps. How many more stamps will fit in the book?

Between _____ and _____ more stamps will fit in the book.

Why? _____

1

Find the Quotient

$487 \div 4 =$ _____

Explain your thinking.

 2

Choose the Correct Answer

With which 3 numbers can you write a true division equation?

A   3, 29, 9

B   5, 10, 55

C   8, 48, 6

D   7, 73, 9

Explain how you know.

3

How Much Money?

Tani saved $5 per week for 1 year. How much money did she save?

Show how you know.

4

True or False?

It takes Rashad 6 min to run $\frac{1}{2}$ mi. True or false? At this rate, it would take him 36 min to run 3 mi.

Show your thinking.

1

Solve

25 × 15¢ = _____

Show your thinking.

2

Choose the Answer

What is the area of a vegetable patch that is 3 ft by 4 ft?

A   7 sq ft

B   10 sq ft

C   12 sq ft

D   14 sq ft

Explain your thinking.

3

What Is Your Story?

Write a story problem for 386 − 93. Show your solution.

4

The Answer Is $1.50

Write at least 6 different equations that have this answer.

Name _____

1

Write the Answers

12,000	324	12,324
+ 8,000	+ 123	+ 8,123

What can you say about these problems? Write three new problems that are related.

2

Choose the Answer

6 ft 7 in. − 3 ft 8 in. = _____

A   3 ft 5 in.

B   3 ft 1 in.

C   2 ft 11 in.

D   2 ft 1 in.

Explain your thinking.

3

How Much Money?

Meliha bought 3 lbs of apples at 59¢ per pound. How much money did Meliha spend?

Explain how you know.

4

True or False?

$850 \div 50 = 16$

Show how you know.

▼ **PARENT NOTE:**
Problems like number 1 give students an opportunity to extend previously developed computation and estimation methods to computation and estimation with larger numbers.

Name that Shape!

Here are the names of 5 different shapes: octagon, triangle, hexagon, quadrilateral, and pentagon.

Here are drawings of the 5 shapes. Write the correct name under each shape.

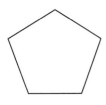   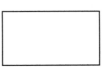

_____   _____   _____

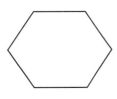

_____   _____

Look around you. Think about shapes you have seen outdoors and in other places. What are 2 different things that have this shape?

1. Triangle _____   _____

2. Quadrilateral _____   _____

3. Pentagon _____   _____

4. Hexagon _____   _____

5. Octagon _____   _____

6. Were any of the shapes you found *equilateral?* If so, which ones?

_____

What's an Easy Way?
Computation Review

Solve these problems as quickly as you can. Use the strategies that work best for you.

Solve.

1. $483 \div 5$

2. $9000 - 16$

3. 8×741

4. $\$6.09 + \$9.95$

5. $\frac{3}{4} + \frac{1}{2}$

6. 13×81

7. $647 + 938$

8. $\$7.25 - \$5.61$

9. $\frac{1}{8} + \frac{1}{8} + \frac{3}{4}$

10. $\frac{7}{8} - \frac{1}{2}$

11. $336 \div 11$

12 . $2372 - 604$

Write the next three numbers in the pattern.

13. 35, 70, 105, _____ , _____ , _____

14. 280, 240, 200, _____ , _____ , _____

15. 5, 10, 20, 40, _____ , _____ , _____

16. 22, 44, 66, _____ , _____ , _____

17. 325, 300, 275, _____ , _____ , _____

Match each problem with the problem in the box that has the same answer.

18. $576 \div 9$

19. $\frac{1}{2}$ of 130

20. 21×3

$693 \div 11$	$148 - 83$	8×8

1 Find the Sum

2 m 62 cm + 1 m 26 cm = _____

Explain your thinking.

2 Choose the Correct Answer

Which has the same answer as
38 + 63 = _____ ?

A   47 + 54 = _____

B   25 + 67 = _____

C   48 + 71 = _____

D   16 + 88 = _____

Explain how you know.

3 How Many Sides?

A hexagon has 6 sides. How
many sides do 9 hexagons have
in all?

Show your thinking.

4 True or False?

400 is a reasonable estimate for
800 – 396.

400 is a reasonable estimate for
600 – 287.

400 is a reasonable estimate for
900 – 412.

Can you write a more reasonable
estimate (not exact answer) for
any of these statements?

1

Find the Quotients

$12\overline{)72}$ $12\overline{)144}$ $12\overline{)288}$

Show your thinking.

2

Which Is False?

A $155 \div 5 = 31$

B $200 \div 5 = 40$

C $115 \div 5 = 23$

D $85 \div 5 = 15$

Explain how you know.

3

True or False?

$\dfrac{4}{6} = \dfrac{2}{3}$

$\dfrac{2}{3} = \dfrac{4}{9}$

$\dfrac{4}{6} = \dfrac{6}{12}$

If any statement is false, change a fraction so that the statement is true.

4

The Area Is 24 Sq Units

Draw at least 2 different rectangles that have this area. Label the dimensions.

Find the Product

82
× 8

Show your thinking.

Choose the Answer

An octagon has 8 sides. How many sides do 7 octagons have in all?

A   15 sides

B   42 sides

C   56 sides

D   72 sides

Explain how you know.

How Many Miles?

Justin's family traveled 829 mi in 3 days. They drove 312 mi the first day and 279 mi the second day. How many miles did they travel on the third day?

Explain your thinking.

True or False?

$3 \times 1500 > 4 \times 1000$

Show how you know.

Polyhedra Jackets

You are given different polyhedra. Find the "jacket" that matches each polyhedron. The jacket shows what a polyhedron looks like when it is "flattened out." Write the letter of the correct jacket next to the polyhedron.

1.  _____

A.

2. 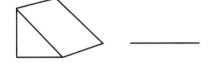 _____

B.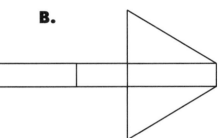

3.  _____

C.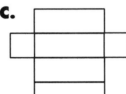

4.  _____

D.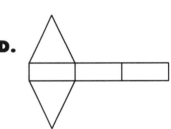

5. 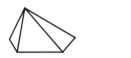 _____

E.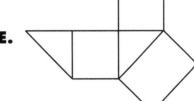

6.  _____

F.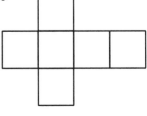

7.  _____

G.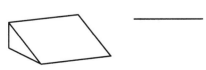

What's Your Strategy?
Convince Me!

Jesse and Jenny's class solved the problem 331 ÷ 40 = _____. Look at their solutions. Notice that Jesse and Jenny got the same, correct answer, but they used different strategies.

Jesse explained his strategy.
The teacher recorded it for the class like this:

331 ÷ 40 = _____

That's about 320 ÷ 40.

320 ÷ 40 = 8

331 - 320 = 11

The answer is 8 R11.

Jenny used a different strategy.
The teacher recorded her explanation like this:

331 ÷ 40 = _____

Count by 40s: 40, 80, 120, 160, 200, 240, 280, 320, 360.

360 is too large.

Use 8 40s = 320

331 - 320 = 11

The answer is 8 R11.

Solve the problems below. Record your explanation on paper.

1. 291 ÷ 70

2. 178 ÷ 20

3. 647 ÷ 80

4. 431 ÷ 60

5. 554 ÷ 90

6. 256 ÷ 40

Name _____

What's the Shape?

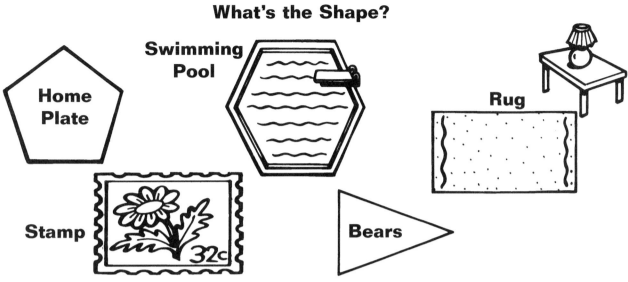

Use the figures to answer the following questions. Fill in the bubble next to the correct answer.

1. Which has the same shape as home plate?

  ○ **A.** triangle   ○ **C.** square

  ○ **B.** pentagon   ○ **D.** hexagon

2. Which has the same shape as the swimming pool?

  ○ **A.** triangle   ○ **C.** square

  ○ **B.** pentagon   ○ **D.** hexagon

3. Which has the same shape as the Bears flag?

  ○ **A.** circle   ○ **C.** triangle

  ○ **B.** pentagon   ○ **D.** hexagon

4. Suppose the rug has two sides that are 6 feet and two sides that are 9 feet. What is its area?

  ○ **A.** 30 square feet

  ○ **B.** 54 square feet

  ○ **C.** 36 square feet

  ○ **D.** 81 square feet

5. What word can be used to name the shape of both the stamp and a football field?

  ○ **A.** quadrilateral   ○ **C.** square

  ○ **B.** trapezoid   ○ **D.** equilateral

Which Shape Fits the Description?

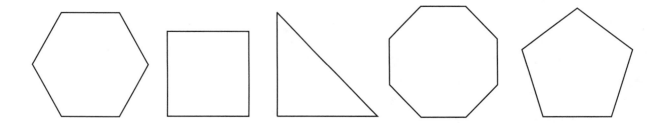

1. Which shape has 4 sides exactly the same length?

2. Which shape has twice as many sides as a square?

3. Suppose you can make two copies of the triangle shown above. Can you combine the two triangles to make one of the other shapes? Explain.

4. Which shape has 1 side less than a hexagon?

5. How many copies of the triangle above would it take to make a hexagon? Sketch your response.

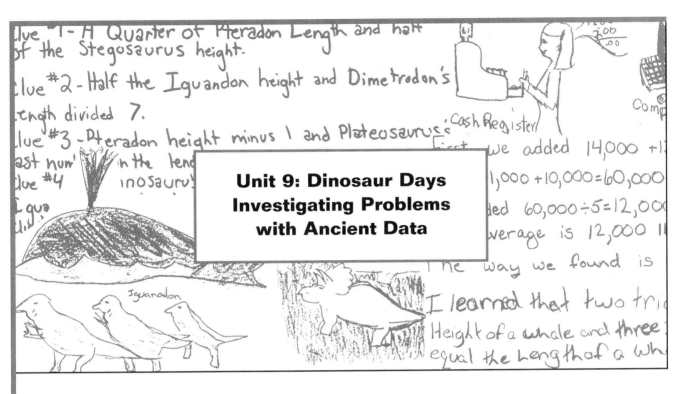

Clue #1 - A Quarter of Pteradon Length and half
of the Stegosaurus height.
Clue #2 - Half the Iguandon height and Dimetrodon's
length divided 7.
Clue #3 - Pteradon height minus 1 and Plateosaurus's
ast nun' in the lend
Clue #4   inosaur

Unit 9: Dinosaur Days
Investigating Problems
with Ancient Data

Cash Register
First we added 14,000 +1
1,000 +10,000 = 60,000
ded 60,000 ÷ 5 = 12,000
verage is 12,000 l
The way we found is
I learned that two tri
Height of a whale and three
equal the Length of a wh

Thinking Questions

What were the dinosaurs really like? How tall were they? How much
did they weigh? Would they fit in your playground? How could you
collect and present data to answer these questions? Can we use this
data to make comparisons between dinosaurs and elephants, or
between dinosaurs and a bus? Or even between dinosaurs and you?

Investigations

This MathLand unit gives you the chance to learn about these ancient
animals and to develop your math skills at the same time. You will
collect data about the dinosaurs and use that data to make
comparisons between different dinosaurs and between dinosaurs and
other objects.

Real-World Math

Research and data collection is an important part of many everyday
activities, whether you're buying a car or going to a restaurant. When
do you use data to help you make decisions?

Name _____

Math Vocabulary

During this MathLand unit, you may be using some of these words as you talk and write about investigations.

A **benchmark** is a point of reference. In this unit, you will use an elephant as a benchmark to visualize the size of a dinosaur.

To get an **average**, the numbers of a set are added together and then divided by the number of members in the set.

Example: The height of five trees are 8 feet, 6 feet, 10 feet, 16 feet, and 20 feet.
8 + 6 + 10 + 16 + 20 = 60 feet
60 ÷ 5 = 12 feet
The average height of the trees is 12 feet.

Database is a collection of data organized in a way that's easy to use. In this unit, you will find data about dinosaurs.

A **cell** is a section of a database spreadsheet. In this unit, there will be cells for writing dinosaurs' height, length, and weight.

A **scale drawing** shows objects larger or smaller than actual size, but the proportion between them remains the same.

Dinosaur Dig

Find all the words in the word bank. When you finish, cross out the Z's that you did not use. Draw a box around all the other letters that were not used and write the letters on the lines to answer the dinosaur riddle.

Word Bank

average
benchmark
database
dinosaur
height
iguanodon
length
maiasaura
plateosaurus
pteranodon
scale drawing
stegosaurus
tons
weigh

P	T	E	R	A	N	O	D	O	N	I	G
L	Z	I	G	U	A	N	O	D	O	N	D
A	R	A	I	G	D	I	N	O	I	S	A
T	U	R	U	E	R	S	Z	W	Z	H	K
E	A	U	Z	G	Z	Z	A	Z	S	T	R
O	S	A	Z	A	Z	R	Z	N	Z	G	A
S	O	S	Z	R	D	Z	O	H	Z	N	M
A	N	A	Z	E	Z	T	H	G	I	E	H
U	I	I	L	V	Z	Z	Z	I	Z	L	C
R	D	A	T	A	B	A	S	E	Z	Z	N
U	C	M	Z	Z	Z	Z	Z	W	Z	Z	E
S	T	E	G	O	S	A	U	R	U	S	B

What did the paleontologist (person who studies fossils) say about his job?

"_ ___ _____!"

1

Find the Products

$$64 \times 21 \qquad 64 \times 20 \qquad 64 \times 22$$

Explain your thinking.

2

Choose the Correct Answer

Four classes will attend the school play. Each class has between 25 and 30 students. The 4 teachers and a few parents will also attend. About how many chairs should Mr. Nakano set up so that everyone has a seat?

A   About 110   C   About 180

B   About 135   D   About 200

Explain how you know.

3

What Is the Perimeter?

A hexagon has 6 sides. If each side is 2 cm long, what is the perimeter of the hexagon?

Show how you know.

4

Which Is Greater?

Put < or > in each circle to show which is greater,

216 ÷ 6 ◯ 205 ÷ 5

192 ÷ 8 ◯ 207 ÷ 9

252 ÷ 6 ◯ 287 ÷ 7

Show how you know.

Multiply

853
× 7

Show your thinking.

Choose the Answer

Imagine that you measured 5 Oviraptors, the dinosaur known as the "egg robber." Two were 6 ft, one was 7 ft, and two were 8 ft long. What is the average length of the 5 Oviraptors?

A   6 ft   C $7\frac{1}{2}$ ft

B   7 ft   D   8 ft

Explain your thinking.

What Fraction?

There are 32 students in Rami's class. Eight students are taking piano lessons. What fraction of the class is taking piano lessons?

Explain how you know.

The Answer Is 15

Write at least 6 different equations that have this answer.

Name _____

Add

436
173
+ 318

Show your thinking.

Choose the Correct Answer

Which problem has a product
of 450?

A   4 × 70 = _____

B   8 × 30 = _____

C   7 × 60 = _____

D   5 × 90 = _____

Explain how you know.

How Many Dinosaurs?

A Tyrannosaurus was about 40 ft
long. How many Tyrannosauruses
lined up head to tail would it take
to reach 320 ft?

Show how you know.

True or False?

Sumi saved $4 per week for
1 year. True or false? Sumi saved
a total of $158.

Explain your thinking.

The Age of Reptiles

Geological Periods

245 mya	208 mya	146 mya	65 mya
Triassic	Jurassic	Cretaceous	

mya = million years ago

1. How long did the Age of Reptiles last? _____

How long was each period within the Age of Reptiles?

2. Triassic _____

3. Jurassic _____

4. Cretaceous _____

5. Plateosaurus lived during the mid-late Triassic Period. About

how many million years ago did Plateosaurus live? _____

6. Stegosaurus lived during the late Jurassic Period. About how

many million years ago did Stegosaurus live? _____

▼ **PARENT NOTE:**
Skill Power provides opportunities to work with many different graphical displays of data. Interpreting graphs is a necessary skill for functioning in an information society in which graphical representation of data is increasingly common.

What's a Good Estimate?
Greater Than, Less Than

Build your estimation skills. For each problem, tell if the answer will be less than (<) or greater than (>) the estimate given. Explain why you think so.

1. 59 × 19 is _____ than 1200 because _____

_____

2. 7 × 852 is _____ than 5700 because _____

_____

3. $\frac{1}{8}$ of 42 is _____ than 5 because _____

_____

4. 784 + 196 is _____ than 1000 because _____

_____

5. 987 − 372 is _____ than 600 because _____

_____

Now, write a problem like one on this page.

1

Subtract

$30.00	$20.00	$50.00
− $17.40	− $15.50	− $34.80

Show your thinking.

2

Choose the Correct Answer

Stanley measured his school playground. Each of the 4 sides was a different length. They measured 72 ft, 66 ft, 21 ft, and 48 ft. What is the perimeter of the playground?

A   187 ft   C   207 ft

B   200 ft   D   227 ft

Show how you know.

3

How Many Books?

Christy and Evan are taking books back to the library. Christy has 14 books. Evan has 8 books. How many books should Christy give Evan so that they each will carry the same number of books?

Explain your thinking.

4

True or False?

10 t = 20,000 lb

40 t = 80,000 lb

80 t = 16,000 lb

Hint: 1 t = 2000 lb

Tell how you know.

PARENT NOTE:
Throughout *Skill Power*, problems such as number 4 are presented to develop students' understanding of patterns and relationships and their ability to use patterns to check computation.

Divide

20) 580

Show your thinking.

Choose the Correct Answer

Find the average of these
numbers: 5, 10, 10, 14, 16, 17.

A   9

B   10

C   12

D   15

Explain your thinking.

True or False?

An Apatosaurus was 70 ft long.
A Hypsilophodon was 7 ft long.
True or false? A Hypsilophodon's
length was $\frac{1}{10}$ the length of
an Apatosaurus.

Explain how you know.

The Answer Is $10

Write at least 6 different
equations that have this answer.

1

Write the Answer

$15.50 ÷ 5 = _____

Show your thinking.

2

Choose the Answer

6 + 79 + 312 = _____

A   385

B   397

C   404

D   412

Show how you know.

3

How Many Pounds?

An Allosaurus weighed $1\frac{1}{2}$ t. How many pounds did an Allosaurus weigh?
Hint: 2000 pounds = 1 ton

Explain how you know.

4

True or False?

The sides of a triangle measure 5 cm each. True or false? The perimeter of the triangle is 15 cm.

Explain your thinking.

How Big Were They?

$\frac{1}{4}$ in. = 4 ft

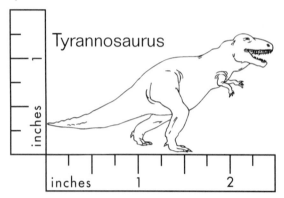

Tyrannosaurus

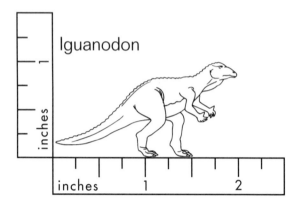

Iguanodon

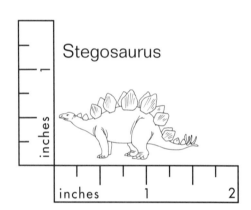

Stegosaurus

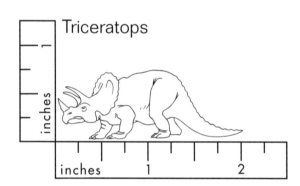

Triceratops

Each of these dinosaurs is drawn to scale. Figure out the approximate dimensions of each dinosaur.

	Length	Height
1. Tyrannosaurus	_____	_____
2. Stegosaurus	_____	_____
3. Triceratops	_____	_____
4. Iguanodon	_____	_____

What's an Easy Way?
Computation Review

Solve these problems as quickly as you can. Use the strategies that work best for you.

Problems 1–8 describe scales used in scale drawings. Complete each statement.

1. If 1 in. = 20 ft, 3 in. = _____

2. If 1 in. = 16 ft, 2 in. = _____

3. If $\frac{1}{2}$ in. = 10 ft, 1 in. = _____

4. If $\frac{1}{2}$ in. = 4 ft, 2 in. = _____

5. If $\frac{1}{4}$ in. = 10 ft, 1 in. = _____

6. If $\frac{1}{4}$ in. = 5 ft, 3 in. = _____

7. If $\frac{1}{2}$ in. = 5 ft, 3 in. = _____

8. If $\frac{1}{4}$ in. = 10 ft, 4 in. = _____

Solve.

9. 435 + 3980

10. 5 × (3 x 4)

11. 234 + 61 + 7

12. $13.25 ÷ 5

13. 3 × $9.79

14. $16.79 − $8.92

15. 3076 − 498

16. 28 × 97

17. 562 ÷ 24

18. 6491 + 1878

19. 486 ÷ 19

20. 5497 − 4839

Find the Differences

78	780	7800
− 12	− 120	− 1200

Show your thinking.

Choose the Correct Answer

With which 3 numbers can you write a true division equation?

A   63, 9, 7

B   72, 8, 7

C   82, 9, 9

D   45, 8, 5

Explain your thinking.

Which Is Greater?

Which is greater, $\frac{1}{8}$ of 16 dinosaur eggs or $\frac{1}{3}$ of 9 dinosaur eggs?

Show how you know.

True or False?

$72 \div 18 = 4$

$144 \div 18 = 6$

$36 \div 18 = 2$

If any statements are false, change them to true statements.

1

Find the Sum

796 + 13 = _____

Explain your thinking.

2

Choose the Correct Answer

Brian brought $10.00 to the school fair. He spent $1.00 at the Ring Toss booth and $2.25 at the Arts and Crafts table. He also bought 3 cookies for $0.35 each. How much money did Brian have left?

A $5.30   C $6.30

B $5.70   D $6.70

Show your thinking.

3

How Long?

The first Iguanodon fossils were found in southern England in 1822. How long has it been since the first Iguanodon fossils were found?

Explain how you know.

4

The Answer Is $5

Write at least 6 different equations that have this answer.

Find the Quotient

$19 \overline{)427}$

Show your thinking.

Choose the Correct Answer

Mr. Tanaka has a piece of pipe that is 625 cm long. How many meters long is the pipe?
Hint: 100 centimeters = 1 meter

A   6 m

B   6 m 25 cm

C   6 m 50 cm

D   60 m

Explain your thinking.

Would They Fit?

An Iguanodon was about 33 ft long. A Triceratops was about 30 ft long. A Plateosaurus was about 26 ft long. Suppose these 3 dinosaurs were lined up head to tail. Would they fit on a 100-ft field?

Explain how you know.

Agree or Disagree?

Carlos has 3 quarters, 4 dimes, and 6 nickels. He says he has enough money to buy a magazine for $1.50. Do you agree or disagree with Carlos?

Show your thinking.

Scale Drawing

Here is a scale drawing of a small pear where 1 cm equals 1 in. Your job is to show the pear's actual size. Look carefully at the sketch of the pear on the 1-cm grid. Use a pencil to sketch the pear as accurately as you can onto the 1-in. grid. (Hint: Think about how the grid might help you make an accurate drawing.)

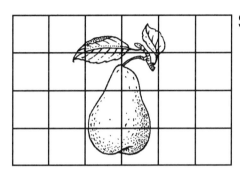

Scale: 1 cm = 1 in.

What's Your Strategy?
Convince Me!

Ernesto and Loren's class solved the problem 771 − 547 = _____ . Look at their solutions. Notice that Ernesto and Loren got the same, correct answer, but they used different strategies.

Ernesto explained his strategy.
The teacher recorded it for the class like this:

Loren used a different strategy.
The teacher recorded her explanation like this:

$$771 - 547 = \underline{\hspace{1cm}}$$

$$547 + 24 = 571$$

$$571 + 200 = 771$$

$$200 + 24 = 224$$

So, $771 - 547 = 224$

$$771 - 547 = \underline{\hspace{1cm}}$$

$$\overset{+3}{774} \overset{+3}{-550}$$

$$700 - 500 = 200$$

$$74 - 50 = 24$$

$$200 + 24 = 224$$

So, $771 - 547 = 224$

Solve the problems below. Record your explanation on paper.

1. 459 − 237

2. 565 − 241

3. 825 − 219

4. 796 − 277

5. 454 − 129

6. 974 − 458

Find the Product

17
× 8

Show your thinking.

Choose the Answer

Mr. Alvarez bought 5 cartons of eggs. There were a dozen eggs in each carton. How many eggs did Mr. Alvarez buy?

A   50 eggs   C   62 eggs

B   60 eggs   D   70 eggs

Explain how you know.

How Many Egg Rolls?

Mr. Ferrar bought 192 egg rolls for a large family reunion. Each package contained 24 egg rolls. How many packages of egg rolls did Mr. Ferrar buy?

Show how you know.

Which Is Greater?

Put < or > in each circle to show which is greater.

$\frac{2}{5}$ ◯ $\frac{2}{2}$

$\frac{4}{8}$ ◯ $\frac{3}{7}$

$\frac{1}{8}$ ◯ $\frac{2}{9}$

Explain your thinking.

1

Subtract

100 − 63 = _____

Explain your thinking.

2

Choose the Best Answer

Round to the nearest foot and add.

6 ft 3 in. + 5 ft 11 in.

A   10 ft   C   12 ft

B   11 ft   D   13 ft

Explain how you know.

3

What Is the Difference?

A baby Mussaurus, or "Mouse Lizard," was only about 8 in. long. The adult Mussaurus was probably about 10 ft long. What was the difference in length between a baby Mussaurus and an adult Mussaurus?

Show your thinking.

4

The Answer Is 3000

Write at least 6 different equations that have this answer.

PARENT NOTE:
When students explain their reasoning about measurement, they have opportunities to develop their understanding of units of measure and to become confident in their ability to use those units.

1

Write the Answers

$15,000 \div 3 =$ _____

$600 \div 2 =$ _____

$4800 \div 8 =$ _____

Explain your strategy for solving these equations.

2

Choose the Correct Answer

Which problem has the greatest sum?

A $42 + 76 =$ _____

B $36 + 57 =$ _____

C $59 + 81 =$ _____

D $93 + 22 =$ _____

Explain how you know.

3

What Is Your Story?

Write a story problem for $3 \times \$1.60$. Show your solution.

4

True or False?

A 4-in.-by-4-in. square has an area of 15 sq in.

Show your thinking.

PARENT NOTE:
In problems such as number 1, students can combine their knowledge of basic facts, such as $15 \div 3$, with their knowledge of place value to compute mentally with multiples of 10, such as 15,000. This is a useful mental math technique.

Agree or Disagree?

This is how Luz solved the problem:

The answer is 4000.
Write at least 6 different equations that have this answer.

Do you agree or disagree with her work? Explain your thinking.

These are a few problems that equal 4000.

①
$$
\begin{array}{r}
4 \\
\times\ 100 \\
\hline
4,000
\end{array}
$$

② $2\overline{)8,000}$ → 4000

③
$$
\begin{array}{r}
4895 \\
-\ 895 \\
\hline
4,000
\end{array}
$$

④
$$
\begin{array}{r}
2,460 \\
+\ 1,540 \\
\hline
4,000
\end{array}
$$

⑤
$$
\begin{array}{r}
2 \\
\times\ 200 \\
\hline
4,000
\end{array}
$$

⑥ $4\overline{)16,000}$ → $4,000$

⑦
$$
\begin{array}{r}
4444 \\
-\ 444 \\
\hline
4,000
\end{array}
$$

⑧
$$
\begin{array}{r}
2,000 \\
+\ 2,000 \\
\hline
4,000
\end{array}
$$

CAN YOU find any more?

What's a Good Estimate?
It's Between ...

Build your estimation skills. For each problem, write two numbers, one number that is greater than and one number that is less than the exact answer would be. Explain why you chose those numbers.

$$\begin{array}{r} 157 \\ \times\ \ 8 \\ \hline \end{array}$$

_____ and _____

Why? _____

_____

$$\begin{array}{r} 825 \\ -343 \\ \hline \end{array}$$

_____ and _____

Why? _____

_____

$4975 \div 6 =$ _____

_____ and _____

Why? _____

_____

$40 \times 67 =$ _____

_____ and _____

Why? _____

_____

The Robinsons drive 915 miles in 20 hours. What is the average number of miles they travel per hour?

They travel between _____ and _____ miles per hour.

Why? _____

1

Multiply

88
× 7

Show your thinking.

2

Choose the Correct Answer

Which sum is an even number?

A   179 + 430 = _____

B   265 + 322 = _____

C   940 + 177 = _____

D   355 + 413 = _____

Explain how you know.

3

How Many Cubes?

Melissa and Ron each have a bag of Rainbow Cubes. Melissa's bag has 25 cubes and Ron's bag has 17 cubes. How many cubes does Melissa need to give Ron so that they will each have the same number? How many cubes will they each have?

Explain your thinking.

4

Which Is Greater?

31 mo $2\frac{1}{2}$ yr

28 mo ◯ $2\frac{1}{2}$ yr

39 mo ◯ 3 yr

37 mo ◯ 3 yr

Explain how you know.

▼1 Write the Answer

$4 \overline{)849}$

Show how you know.

▼2 Choose the Correct Answer

Which has the same answer as
$4 \times 81 = $ _____ ?

A $5 \times 72 = $ _____

B $3 \times 99 = $ _____

C $8 \times 26 = $ _____

D $6 \times 54 = $ _____

Explain how you know.

▼3 The Permian Period

The time just before the dinosaurs appeared, when reptiles were taking over from amphibians, is called the Permian Period. The Permian Period lasted from about 290 million years ago to 245 million years ago. How long did the Permian Period last?

Explain your thinking.

▼4 The Answer Is 6 Ft

Write at least 6 different equations that have this answer.

1

Find the Differences

$$
\begin{array}{r} 2931 \\ -\ 2756 \\ \hline \end{array}
\qquad
\begin{array}{r} 7391 \\ -\ 7186 \\ \hline \end{array}
\qquad
\begin{array}{r} 5561 \\ -\ 5277 \\ \hline \end{array}
$$

Explain your thinking.

2

Choose the Correct Answer

Every other day Ali makes dinner. About how many days each year does he make dinner?

A   About 180 days

B   About 200 days

C   About 220 days

D   About 365 days

Explain how you know.

3

How Long?

A Saltasaurus was about 40 ft long. A Stygimoloch was about $\frac{1}{5}$ the length of a Saltasaurus. About how long was a Stygimoloch?

Show your thinking.

4

True or False?

After the fourth-grade pizza party, there were 18 thirds of pizza left. True or false? That is equivalent to 4 whole pizzas.

Show your thinking.

PARENT NOTE:

When working with fractions, students use a variety of techniques, including using pictures and diagrams to solve problems. Ask your child to explain how he or she solves problems such as number 3 and number 4.

Comparison Clues

Read each clue and write the letter of the object it describes.

Dinosaur Dimensions		
	Length	Height
Compsognathus	3 ft	8 in.
Kentrosaurus	15 ft	4 ft
Allosaurus	24 ft	7 ft
Spinosaurus	40 ft	9 ft

1. This object is $\frac{1}{5}$ the length of Kentrosaurus and

3 times the height of Compsognathus. _____

A.

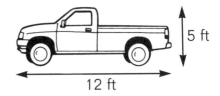

5 ft

12 ft

2. This object is $\frac{1}{2}$ the length of Compsognathus and

$\frac{1}{2}$ the height of Allosaurus. _____

B.

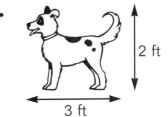

2 ft

3 ft

3. This object is $\frac{1}{4}$ the length of Allosaurus and about

$\frac{1}{2}$ the height of Spinosaurus. _____

C.

5 ft

6 ft

4. This object is $\frac{1}{2}$ the length of Allosaurus and 4 ft

shorter than Spinosaurus. _____

D.

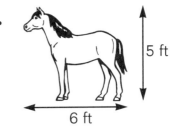

$3\frac{1}{2}$ ft

$1\frac{1}{2}$ ft

What's an Easy Way?
Computation Review

Solve these problems as quickly as you can. Use the strategies that work best for you.

Solve.

1. $\frac{1}{2}$ of 8

2. $\frac{1}{3}$ of 6

3. $\frac{1}{4}$ of 8

4. $\frac{1}{2}$ of 12

5. $\frac{1}{5}$ of 15

6. $\frac{1}{3}$ of 12

7. $\frac{1}{5}$ of 10

8. $\frac{1}{4}$ of 16

9. $\frac{1}{2}$ of 20

Solve.

10. $329 \div 3$

11. $3456 - 3282$

12. 9×58

13. $3 \times \$5.19$

14. $493 \div 70$

15. $\$20.01 - \$7.64$

16. $4107 + 2398$

17. 19×48

18. $631 \div 6$

19. 12×75

20. $\$16.94 + \$12.01$

▼ **PARENT NOTE:**
Learning to communicate one's thinking and to consider other students' strategies are skills that students will develop throughout the year as they write about and discuss their ways of solving computation problems.

How High Is It?

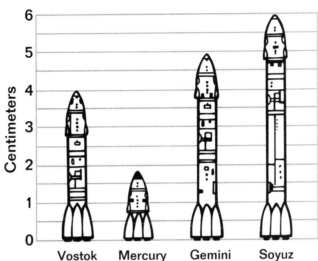

1 cm = 4 ft

Use the graph to answer the following questions. Fill in the bubble next to the correct answer.

1. About how many feet high is the *Vostok?*

   ○ **A.** about 8 ft   ○ **C.** about 12 ft

   ○ **B.** about 16 ft   ○ **D.** about 24 ft

2. About how many feet high is the *Gemini?*

   ○ **A.** about 7 ft   ○ **C.** about 15 ft

   ○ **B.** about 19 ft   ○ **D.** about 23 ft

3. The *Soyuz* is about how many feet higher than the *Mercury?*

   ○ **A.** about 7 ft   ○ **C.** about 12 ft

   ○ **B.** about 20 ft   ○ **D.** about 17 ft

4. An *Apollo* Command Module is about $1\frac{1}{2}$ times as high as the *Soyuz.* About how high is that?

   ○ **A.** about 12 ft   ○ **C.** about 30 ft

   ○ **B.** about 36 ft   ○ **D.** about 48 ft

5. An *Apollo* Lunar Module is between 3 and 4 times as high as a *Mercury.* About how high is that? Choose the closest estimate.

   ○ **A.** less than 21 feet

   ○ **B.** more than 28 feet

   ○ **C.** between 21 and 28 feet

   ○ **D.** none of these choices

What's the Average?

Pounds of Newspapers Recycled

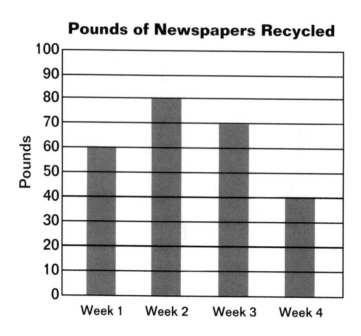

The graph shows the amount of newspaper recycled each week. Use the graph to answer the questions.

1. How many pounds of newspaper are recycled in all during the four weeks?

2. What is the average amount of newspaper recycled each week?

3. Suppose 30 more pounds of newspaper were recycled during Week 2 and 10 more pounds were recycled Week 4. What would the new average for the four weeks be?

4. Suppose 10 fewer pounds of newspaper were recycled during Week 2 and 10 fewer pounds were recycled Week 4. What would the new average for the four weeks be?

5. How does adding to the total number of pounds change the average? How does subtracting from the total number of pounds change the average?

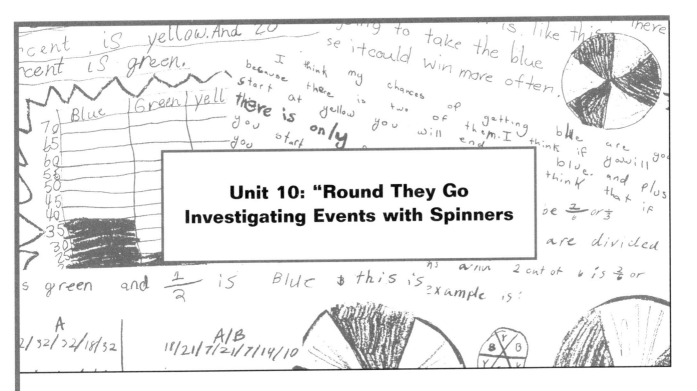

Thinking Questions

How can you model probability using a spinner? How can you determine whether a spinner game is fair or unfair? What happens to the outcomes of a spin when you change the sizes of the spinner's sections? Can you make colors more or less likely to occur? What kinds of games can you create that use spinners?

Investigations

In this MathLand unit, you will use spinners to investigate the concepts of probability. You will learn how changing the spinner space changes the likelihood of the outcomes. You will use fraction language to talk about probabilities and you will design and play your own carnival games based on spinners and probability.

Real-World Math

You will find probability being used in everyday life. The newspaper is full of people predicting the probability, or likelihood, of certain events happening—events such as a hurricane, a stock market crash, or even who will win the next World Series. Have you used probability to try to predict the outcome of an event recently?

Math Vocabulary

During this MathLand unit, you may be using some of these words as you talk and write about probability.

Probability is the chance that something will happen. In this unit, you will play games and do experiments to explore probability.

You can make a **prediction** based on what you know or observe.

Example: The cafeteria will be crowded today since they are giving away free pizza.

A game is **fair** when all players have an equal chance of winning.

A game is **unfair** when some players have a better chance of winning than others.

Probability Pyramid

What is the probability of a pyramid being built upside-down? Not much! However, lucky you have the chance to climb it. Use the word "Probability" to come up with words to fill in the upside-down pyramid. Add up the value of each letter to get your score. There are several words that will fit in the spaces; the trick is to use the letters that will give you the most points.

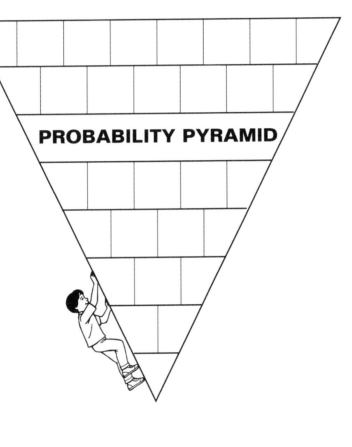

	P	R	O	B	A	B	I	L	I	T	Y
value of each letter:	4	5	2	3	1	3	2	5	2	3	4

8 letter word

7 letter word

PROBABILITY PYRAMID

5 letter word

4 letter word

3 letter word

2 letter word

1 letter word

Total

1 Write the Answers

(Hint: In problems such as these, mathematicians have agreed to solve inside the parentheses first.)

$3 \times 4 \times 5 \times 6 =$ _____

$(3 \times 4) \times (5 \times 6) =$ _____

$3 \times (4 \times 5) \times 6 =$ _____

$(3 \times 5) \times (4 \times 6) =$ _____

From these problems, what can you say about multiplying a series of numbers?

2 Choose the Correct Answer

Which problem has a quotient of 30?

A $80 \div 4 =$ _____

B $60 \div 3 =$ _____

C $90 \div 3 =$ _____

D $70 \div 2 =$ _____

Explain your thinking.

3 The Dime Toss

Shanti played the Dime Toss game at her school fair. For every dime that lands in the jar, she gets 3 dimes back. She loses the dimes that do not land in the jar. Shanti tossed a total of 12 dimes. Three landed in the jar and the others missed. Does Shanti have more or less money than she started with? How much more or less money does she have?

Explain how you know.

4 True or False?

The answer is greater than $100. True or false?

$72.90 + $28.75

$57.30 + $41.96

$63.99 + $36.99

$48.01 + $51.49

Could you decide whether the answer was greater than $100.00 without finding the exact answer? Explain your thinking.

PARENT NOTE:
The ability to estimate whether a sum of two or more money amounts is greater than a particular amount is an important skill used in everyday situations.

Find the Sum

```
  3708
   416
+   85
─────
```

Show your thinking.

Choose the Correct Answer

The elevator holds 1050 lb, maximum. Can 7 people with an average weight of 140 lb each ride safely at the same time?

A   No, they weigh too much.

B   Yes, they weigh exactly 1050 lb.

C   Yes, they weigh 20 lb under the limit.

D   Yes, they weigh 70 lb under the limit.

True or False?

(Hint: 60 min = 1 h)

120 min = 2 h

240 min = 3 h

480 min = 8 h

If any statements are false, change them to true statements.

The Answer Is 720

Write at least 6 different equations that have this answer.

1

Solve

$\frac{5}{8} + \frac{4}{8} =$ _____

Explain your thinking.

2

Choose the Answer

$13{,}000 \div 13 =$ _____

A   10

B   100

C   1000

D   10,000

Explain how you know.

3

What Is the Answer?

Take 6. Double it. Multiply your answer by 3. Divide that answer by 2. What is the answer?

Show your thinking.

4

True or False?

Talia bought a package of a dozen tortillas. Over the course of the week, she used $\frac{1}{4}$ of them. True or false? Talia had 9 tortillas left.

Show how you know.

Likely or Unlikely?

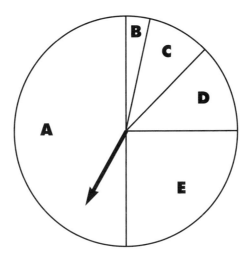

Look carefully at the spinner and answer True or False to each question.

Suppose you spin the arrow 1 time.

1. It is likely that it will land on A.

2. It is unlikely that it will land on B.

3. It is very likely that it will land on C.

Choose one of your answers above and explain your thinking.

Suppose you spin the arrow 100 times.

4. It will land on A about $\frac{1}{2}$ of the time.

5. It will land on B about $\frac{1}{3}$ of the time.

6. It will land on D about $\frac{1}{8}$ of the time.

7. It will land on E about $\frac{1}{4}$ of the time.

Choose one of your answers above and explain your thinking.

8. Write 2 more True-or-False questions for your classmates to answer. Be sure to have your solutions ready.

What's a Good Estimate?
Greater Than, Less Than

Build your estimation skills. For each problem, tell if the answer will be less than (<) or greater than (>) the estimate given. Explain why you think so.

1. $\frac{1}{4}$ of 50 is _____ than 12 because _____

_____

2. 809 ÷ 19 is _____ than 40 because _____

_____

3. $\frac{1}{3}$ of 32 is _____ than 11 because _____

_____

4. 3718 − 1906 is _____ than 2000 because _____

_____

5. $\frac{1}{5}$ of 34 is _____ than 6 because _____

_____

Now, write a problem like one on this page.

1

Write the Answer

```
  646
×   3
```

Show your thinking.

2

Choose the Closest Estimate

Kelly rides her bike 3 times per week for a total of about 100 km. Which is the closest estimate of the average distance Kelly rides each time?

A   25 km   C   33 km

B   30 km   D   40 km

Explain how you know.

3

How Many Birds?

There are 17 birds in the tree and 13 birds on the ground. There are some more birds on the fence. There are 41 birds all together. How many birds are on the fence?

Explain your thinking.

4

True or False?

(Hint: 1 mile = 5280 ft)

$\frac{1}{2}$ mi = 2640 ft

$\frac{1}{4}$ mi = 1320 ft.

$\frac{1}{8}$ mi = 330 ft

If any statements are false, change them to true statements.

PARENT NOTE:
Students encounter the concept of averages in their daily lives. At school, they can build upon these experiences as they discuss situations involving averages,

1. Find the Quotients

$75 \div 7 =$ _____

$64 \div 6 =$ _____

$87 \div 8 =$ _____

Show your thinking.

2. Choose the Correct Answer

Five is what fraction of 35?

A $\frac{1}{5}$

B $\frac{1}{7}$

C $\frac{1}{8}$

D $\frac{1}{10}$

Explain how you know.

3. How Many Times?

Mr. Chui took a 2-week vacation. While he was gone, Mr. Chui had Eva walk his dog twice a day. How many times did Eva walk Mr. Chui's dog?

Explain your thinking.

4. The Answer Is 85¢

Write at least 6 different equations that have this answer.

1

Divide

$5\overline{)625}$

Show your thinking.

2

Choose the Answer

Gloria scored 12 points in last night's basketball game. She scored $\frac{1}{6}$ of her team's points. How many total points did the team score?

A 24 points   C 72 points

B 36 points   D 84 points

Explain your thinking.

3

Which Size?

Corn Crunchies are on sale. The 10-oz size is $1.60. The 24-oz size is $3.36. Which size would you buy to get the most for your money?

Show how you know.

4

True or False?

A can of cat food costs $1.20. True or false? You can buy 9 cans with a ten-dollar bill.

Explain how you know.

PARENT NOTE:
When students explain their thinking in problem number 3, they have the opportunity to clarify their thoughts on choosing the better buy. This helps them develop their reasoning processes and their confidence with a skill used in daily life.

Central School Carnival Spinners

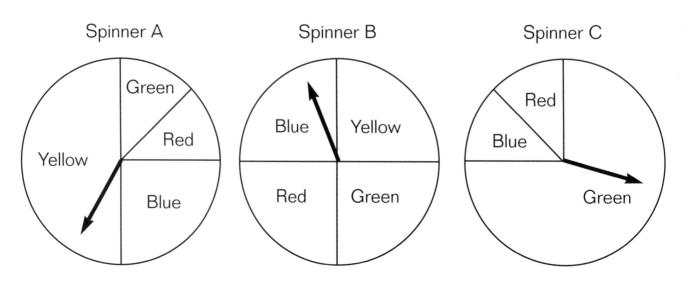

Spinner A   Spinner B   Spinner C

The Central School Carnival raises money for local charities. At the carnival this year, there are three games that use spinners. Look carefully at each spinner and answer these questions.

1. At Spinner A, you win a prize by landing on yellow. You do not win if you land on green, red, or blue. Is this game fair? Explain your thinking.

2. Suppose you need to land on blue to win a game. With which spinner are you least likely to win? Explain your thinking.

3. Suppose you need to land on red to win. With which spinner are you most likely to win? Explain how you know.

4. Suppose you need to land on green to win. Use a fraction to describe your chances of winning with each spinner.

What's an Easy Way?
Computation Review

Solve these problems as quickly as you can. Use the strategies that work best for you.

Solve.

1. $\frac{2}{3} + \frac{1}{3}$

2. $\frac{1}{4} + \frac{1}{8}$

3. $\frac{3}{4} - \frac{1}{2}$

4. $1 - \frac{2}{3}$

5. $\frac{3}{4} + \frac{1}{8} + \frac{1}{8}$

6. $\frac{1}{8} + \frac{3}{4}$

7. $\frac{1}{5} + \frac{3}{10}$

8. $\frac{3}{4} - \frac{1}{8}$

9. $1 - \frac{3}{8}$

Put < or > in each ◯ to show which is greater.

10. $\frac{1}{4}$ ◯ $\frac{1}{2}$

11. $\frac{5}{8}$ ◯ $\frac{1}{2}$

12. $\frac{2}{3}$ ◯ $\frac{5}{6}$

Solve.

13. 4×518

14. $96 \div 7$

15. $8 \times \$1.45$

16. $724 \div 4$

17. 21×34

18. $\$12.39 \div 3$

19. $6 \times \$3.03$

20. $146 \div 6$

What's Your Strategy?
Convince Me!

Bruce and Kate solved the problem $\frac{3}{8} + \frac{3}{4} =$ _____ . Look at their solutions.
Notice that Bruce and Kate got the same, correct answer, but they used
different strategies.

Bruce explained his strategy.
The teacher recorded it for the class
like this:

$$\frac{3}{8} + \frac{3}{4} = \underline{\hphantom{xx}}$$

$$\frac{3}{8} = \frac{1}{4} + \frac{1}{8}$$

$$\frac{1}{4} + \frac{3}{4} + \frac{1}{8} = 1\frac{1}{8}$$

Kate used a different strategy.
The teacher recorded her explanation
like this:

$$\frac{3}{8} + \frac{3}{4} = \underline{\hphantom{xx}}$$

$$\frac{3}{4} = \frac{6}{8}$$

$$\frac{3}{8} + \frac{6}{8} = \frac{9}{8}$$

$$\frac{9}{8} = 1\frac{1}{8}$$

Solve the problems below. Record your explanation on paper.

1. $\frac{3}{10} + \frac{3}{5}$

2. $\frac{3}{4} + \frac{5}{8}$

3. $\frac{5}{6} + \frac{2}{3}$

4. $\frac{1}{4} + \frac{3}{8}$

5. $\frac{2}{3} + \frac{4}{9}$

6. $\frac{1}{2} + \frac{7}{8}$

What's a Good Estimate?
It's Between ...

Problem solvers estimate as a way to check that their final solutions are reasonable. Build your estimation skills. For each problem, write the two numbers that the answer is between. Then explain why those numbers make sense.

```
   3459
  +2357
```

_____ and _____

Why? _____

_____

```
  $9.85
 ×    3
```

_____ and _____

Why? _____

_____

$2238 - 754 =$ _____

_____ and _____

Why? _____

_____

$89 ÷ 8 =$ _____

_____ and _____

Why? _____

_____

The class sells 16 raffle tickets. Each ticket costs $2.75. How much money does the class collect?

They collect between _____ and _____

Why? _____

Which Spinner Do You Choose?

At the fair, there are three spinners. Use the spinner to answer the questions.

Spinner A 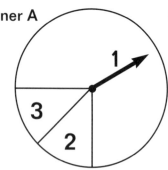 Spinner B 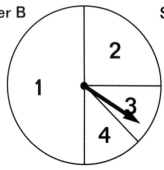 Spinner C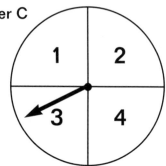

Fill in the bubble next to the correct answer.

1. Which spinner gives you an equal chance of spinning any of the 4 numbers?

   ○ **A.** Spinner A   ○ **C.** Spinner C

   ○ **B.** Spinner B   ○ **D.** None of the spinners

2. Which spinner would you choose if you wanted to have the best chance possible of spinning a 1?

   ○ **A.** Spinner A   ○ **C.** Spinner C

   ○ **B.** Spinner B   ○ **D.** None of the spinners

3. Which spinner would you *not* choose if you wanted the best possible chance of spinning a 2?

   ○ **A.** Spinner A   ○ **C.** Spinner C

   ○ **B.** Spinner B   ○ **D.** None of the spinners

4. On which spinner is your chance of spinning 1 equal to $\frac{1}{2}$?

   ○ **A.** Spinner A   ○ **C.** Spinner C

   ○ **B.** Spinner B   ○ **D.** None of the spinners

5. On which spinner is your chance of spinning 4 equal to $\frac{1}{8}$?

   ○ **A.** Spinner A   ○ **C.** Spinner C

   ○ **B.** Spinner B   ○ **D.** None of the spinners

How Likely Is it?

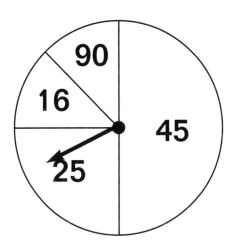

Children at the fair played a game with this spinner. Use the spinner to answer the questions.

1. Suppose you spin this spinner 100 times. Which number do you think you will spin the most times?

2. Suppose you spin 100 times. Which two numbers do you think you will spin about the same number of times?

3. Suppose you spin 100 times. Which number do you think you will spin about twice as often as 90?

4. Jorge spins 90, 45, and 45. What is the average number of points that he gets per spin?

5. Tara spins 3 times. The sum of these 3 spins is 86. What 3 numbers does she spin?